To

Denis.

CW00857305

CHRONICLES OF THE NEWDEGATES AND THE THREE MANORS

with

best wishes

Roy Wilkinson.

Arbury Hall

CHRONICLES OF THE NEWDEGATES AND THE THREE MANORS

Roy Wilkinson

ATHENA PRESS
LONDON

ISBN 1 84401 771 0

First Published 2006 by
ATHENA PRESS
Queen's House, 2 Holly Road
Twickenham TW1 4EG
United Kingdom

Printed for Athena Press

*25 November 2006 is the 200th anniversary
of the death of Sir Roger Newdigate,
Fifth Baronet of Arbury, Warwickshire.*

*This work is dedicated to him; a celebration of the
lifetime of a truly innovative and
remarkable character, whose achievements enhance the
lives of all of us to this day.*

Acknowledgements

Many kind people have supported the production of this book and to them all I owe a great debt of gratitude.

First I must sincerely thank the fourth Viscount Daventry for his enthusiastic involvement from the beginning, in the form of proofreading and supplying family details that were previously guarded family secrets, and above all for his generous sponsorship.

A text of this nature must benefit enormously from the involvement of the main man, and this is certainly no exception. So a very big thank you is in order to the present Viscount Daventry and especially so for loaning me the use of family portraits and indeed for the whole of his contribution.

Two other invaluable friends that made this production possible in the first instance are husband and wife team Bailey and Pauline Bevins, who have been generously involved throughout.

Without their encouragement I would never have started, so I owe them an immense debt of gratitude, especially for their part so well done.

Another four colleagues, Jim Wagstaff, Paul Wynne, Bill Mathews and Steve Wilcox, all made significant contributions to the production. To them I am also indebted.

I have also benefited from the kind support of many other people too numerous to mention; here are just a few:

Miss Brenda Newell (Arbury), Miss Jean Lapworth, Mrs Margaret Chessum (Eyeworth Bedfordshire), Mrs Jane Mennell (Harefield, Middlesex), Rev. A J R Gandon BA (St Mary's Church, Harefield, Middlesex), Mr Nicholas Gibbs (Cambridgeshire), Robert Higginbottom and *Coventry Evening Telegraph*, historian Mr David McGrory for his ghost story, all the hard-working staff at Nuneaton library, and last, but by no means least, I acknowledge all the other authors who have generously supplied me with facts during extensive research – to them a huge thank you.

And finally thank you to Viscountess Daventry, who unwittingly gave me the idea in the first place.

Foreword

I would like to express great thanks and admiration for Roy Wilkinson's fascinating gallop through the Newdegate history.

He has managed to demystify and untangle the complex family history, as well as the changing faces of three manors and of Arbury itself.

My wife and I have so enjoyed reading of the progression throughout the ages, and to have such a comprehensive and interesting record is for us invaluable. We feel so privileged to live in such a magnificent house within such an historic park and hope that the story may continue for many more generations to come.

The Rt Hon. The Viscount Daventry

The Rt Hon. The Viscount Daventry with his son and heir, Humphrey.
Photograph by kind permission of Mr Hugo Burnand.

The author, Roy Wilkinson

Introduction

I believe my fascination for Arbury goes back to my childhood during those austere years following the end of the second world war when as a youngster I would accompany my grandfather through the Round Towers gateway along North Walk to attend the meet of the Atherstone hunt.

Just walking beneath Sir Roger Newdegate's grandiose archway felt as though I was entering another world. It was a very beautiful and mysterious place; my lifelong love affair with Arbury had begun.

The meet itself was indeed a very lively and colourful occasion, which would often take place on the Avenue at the top of the hill on North Walk, amidst beautiful mellow tints of autumn colour.

Sometimes we would walk further to try and follow the progress of the hunt. I remember on one occasion standing on Somerlands Bridge and seeing the defunct Prisoner of War camp in the park, with its many desolate huts littering the fields. It was quite an eerie and depressing scene.

My earliest memories of the Hall itself go back to the mid-fifties when as a teenager I became inquisitive about the interior of this fairytale palace.

I remember vividly the late Hon. Mrs Lucia Charlotte Susan FitzRoy Newdegate sitting proudly in the entrance hall welcoming all the visitors in person, for in those days they arrived in their droves.

I made many return visits in subsequent years and, although I was not aware of it at the time, my insatiable appetite for local history had been aroused.

Listening to the well-informed guides in the Hall fuelled my imagination, while from the late sixties onwards partridge walking and beating on the pheasant shoot earned me freedom to walk the estate. This allowed me to get to know well our beautiful countryside around Arbury and Astley; walking was always and still is a real passion.

In 1990 during the end-of-the-season Arbury shoot dinner, my gamekeeper friend Owen Stainthorpe introduced me to Arbury Administrator Colonel Major David Morris-Barker. He recognised my interest and a new guide to the Hall was born.

Since then I have felt privileged to work at Arbury Hall whilst enjoying its unique beauty and learning more of its hidden past in the process.

Equally, my local walking stirred my imagination during my visits to the beautiful village of Astley, where I longed to know more about the historically famous church and castle.

For a place of its size Astley has a quite magnificent past with its royal connections making national news, while its more down-to-earth links with the Newdegate family give it a glorious history. It is a place of rare beauty and mystical intrigue.

During a visit to Harefield and its Church of St Mary the Virgin in September 1995 I had the privilege to meet church secretary Mrs Jane Mennell who was most knowledgeable about the Middlesex village and its past lords of the manor. Mrs Mennell, who was a cousin of the late third Viscount Daventry, described herself as the last of the Newdegates in Harefield. Jane spent her childhood living at Arbury Hall where she knew the owner, Sir Francis Alexander Newdigate-Newdegate, as Uncle Frank. After leaving Arbury in 1927, Mrs Mennell has lived at Harefield ever since, and is obviously very proud and knowledgeable of her past. I had the perfect guide for my visit to Harefield church that day, which is virtually a mausoleum for the Newdegate family. It proved to be a most interesting and enlightening visit.

So with all this interest, a document recording a history of all three manors entwined by the Newdegate family was eventually conceived.

It is a brief chronological order of events which have made national news down to simple everyday occurrences from Domesday through to the beginning of the twenty-first century, on all three country estates.

The thesis of the *Chronicles of the Newdegates and the Three*

Manors is so vast a playing field, one could keep researching and compiling indefinitely. Most historians, I'm aware, could add something different, but it is impossible to know or include everything as the text flits from place to place.

I hope it's a useful document and a fairly comprehensive record for future generations to understand more about the Newdegates and the historical events concerning the manors in which they have lived.

Contents

Mists of Time

Arbury, or Erdbury as it was known at the time of Domesday, once lay close to the northern edge of the ancient Forest of Arden. In those days it was an area very sparsely populated, though occupation in Roman times was revealed by the discovery of kilns for firing roofing tiles and cooking bowls made from local clay.

In 1087, most of the hamlet of Griff and Chilvers Coton belonged to Harold de Sudeley, whose manor house, of which all traces have long gone, was situated close to what is now the Griff House hotel traffic island on the A444. During the reign of Henry II (1154–1189) Harold's grandson Ralph de Sudeley was Lord of Griff. During this period it became fashionable for rich people to give segments of land to the order of the Knights Templars who were fighting the crusades.

Religious orders also benefited as Ralph gave land to the Augustinian Canons who in time built Erdbury Priory. Probably only a small number of Canons would have occupied the Priory during an era which lasted until the dissolution of the monasteries over 350 years later.

The order of the Knights Templars was founded in 1119.

One and a half miles south-west of Erdbury lay a clearing in the forest known as Eastlea. It appears to have been created during the Saxon period and towards the end of this era flourished under a Saxon lord named Alsi. The Saxon reign was coming to an end with the defeat of King Harold by William the Conqueror in 1066. Gradually the whole country fell under Norman rule and a lot of land in the Astley or Eastlea area was granted under feudal tenure to the Earl of Leicester and subsequently fell into the hands of Phillip de Astley.

The family took their name from the place and the manor remained in their possession until late into the fourteenth century.

It was during this period that some of the most important events connected with Astley took place.

In the *Domesday Book* the section referring to Astley reads:

Estleia I hide and Godric of him.
    There is land for two ploughs. In the demesne is 1 plough, and
5 villeins and 3 borders with 1 plough. There is a wood 1 league
long and half a league broad when it bears (onerat) it is worth 10
shillings. It [the estate] is worth 20 shillings. Alsi held it freely.

The name of Harefield in the county of Middlesex is first found
in Saxon times when Harefelle Moor was already known as a
hunting ground for bears, wolves and other animals. The Saxons
however were not the first to settle there, and flint implements
dating back to Neolithic and Palaeolithic times over 10,000 years
ago were found near the river Colne. There are also signs of an
Iron Age settlement to the east, and more recently a minor
Roman road was discovered running through the village from St
Albans to the river Thames near Laleham.

The *Domesday Book* tells us that Richard, son of Gilbert Earl of
Briou, holds Harefelle with an annual value of £12. It was worth
more before William's men inflicted much damage on the area
prior to entering London in 1066. The great book also tells us that
Richard FitzGilbert also held the Manor of Harefelle and its
administration area of Clare. This connection with the Clare
family lasted until late in the twelfth century. Some of the oldest
stones in Harefield Church date from the twelfth century, but
there was a priest at Harefield in 1086 so it was more than likely
that earlier a wooden church stood on the spot. The priest whose
name was Robert at the time of Domesday was appointed by the
Knights Hospitallers at Moor Hall. Just like Astley, Harefield
Church is dedicated to St Mary the Virgin, with most of the
present structure dating from the thirteenth and fourteenth
centuries, though additions and improvements have been added
during every century since.

Inevitably, the major theme of the church is the history of
Harefield's past lords of the manor, and it became the final resting
place for most of them.

More than twenty monuments decorate St Mary's of the
Newdegate family. In fact the oldest memorial in the building is a
brass to the wife of William Newdegate, Editha, who died in 1444.

The twelfth-century St Mary the Virgin, Harefield

Augustinian Canons of Erdbury

Around the year 1200, when Erdbury Priory (Arbury) was comparatively new, there were 165 Augustinian monasteries in England.

The order of St Augustine was introduced about the year 1100, and members of the order were known as 'regular canons' living under a rule of life based upon the writings of St Augustine (AD 345-430).

They would have been presided over by a prior who lived in his own house; under him was a sub-prior who acted as a deputy in the prior's absence. Other officers such as a cellarer looked after catering; a sacrint looked after the church. The canon's clothes were managed by the chamberlain, while the hosteller looked after the needs of guests.

Canons would spend some time each day reading and writing in the cloisters, which was normally surrounded by all the other buildings: the church to the north, the dormitory and chapter house to the east, a refectory on the southside with stores and servants' quarters to the west.

At most Augustinian establishments worship normally occupied about eight hours each day.

During the Middle Ages there were around 900 monastic buildings in England.

Plantagenet Era

1170

The first castle was built at Astley by Phillip de Astley.

1181–85

Beatrice de Bollers, along with her son Geoffrey, held the Manor of Harefield.

1199

Start of the reign of King John. The Newdegate family tree can be traced back to this period. The family appear to have taken their name from the village of Newdigate in Surrey.

1265

The Astleys temporarily lost possession of Astley when Thomas was slain on 4 August at the battle of Evesham, during the Barons War against Henry III. Simon de Montford was killed along with eighteen barons, 150 knights and 4,000 soldiers.

Henry III took pity on Thomas's widow Edith and soon allowed her a small part of the estate back. Edith's eldest son Andrew redeemed the greater part after winning the King's favour for his role in Palestine during the Crusades.

1285

First mention of a church at Astley. Stephen de Astley was the incumbent.

1301

The death of Andrew de Astley; he was succeeded by his son Nicholas.

1309

During June, King Edward II spent one night at Griff Templars Manor on the way from London to Chester, a journey he made to meet a royal friend, Piers Gaveston, who was returning to England after being exiled in Ireland. On the return the King stayed at Merevale Abbey and Coventry when he made his way through the area.

1312

Order of the Knights Templars was disbanded and the Knights Hospitallers took over at Griff.

1314

Nicholas de Astley went to aid Edward III in his invasion of Scotland. He was taken prisoner and does not appear to have returned.

He was succeeded by his nephew Thomas.

1315

The Manor of Harefield conveyed to Simon de Swanland.

1343

Sir Thomas de Astley founded and built what he described as a fair and beautiful Collegiate church, which he dedicated to St Mary the Virgin.

Built on the site of an earlier church, it took the form of a cross with a central tower. The tower was surmounted with a lead-covered spire from which a light was hung. This was known as the lantern of Arden and guided travellers through the Forest of Arden after dark.

1346

Edward III granted the Newdegate family crest of the Fleur de Lys to Sir John Newdegate for his valiant efforts at the Battle of Crecy.

1354

During this time the de Swanlands owned a park at Harefield known as Homepark.

1357

It is recorded that Joanne, granddaughter of Roger de Bacheworth and daughter of Simon de Swanland, became heiress of the Manor of Harefield upon the death of her three brothers, and married Sir John Newdegate, brother of William de Newdegate of Surrey.

1378

Thomas de Brackenburgh, who held the lease of Harefield, became a Knight of the Shire of Middlesex.

However, towards the end of this century William de Swanland granted a lease of sixty years for land to William Brekspere, who also received other leases after this time.

1383

John de Plumpton was incumbent at the new Collegiate church at Astley and he saw the church through the early fifteenth century when John Milner took over.

1400–1430

(A4) As we come to the fifteenth century the Augustinian canons went quietly about their business at Erdbury. Small establishments like this were usually managed by just a few canons looking after the needs of travellers, the sick and the needy, whilst tending the countryside.

(B8) During this period Joanna Astley, who was the last in the family line, married Reginald Lord Grey and to them a son was born. In time their son married the only daughter of Earl Ferrars of Groby, and afterwards became Lord Grey of Groby. And so the Manor of Astley passed into the Grey family.

The oldest brass in Harefield. Editha Newdegate (d. 1444), wife of William Newdegate, Harefield.

1437

Elizabeth Woodville (Widville), a future wife of Lord John Grey of Astley, was born to Sir Richard Wydville and his wife Princess Jaquetta of Luxembourg. Elizabeth, the eldest of sixteen children, was also a future wife of the Yorkist King Edward IV.

1440–1450s

To the Greys of Astley two sons were born named John and Edward. The younger son Edward was responsible for building the Lady Chapel at Astley, while later John became Lord of the Manor of Astley for a time following his marriage to Elizabeth Woodville.

On most historic documents the name of the Woodvilles is spelt in various ways, i.e. Wydville, Wydeville, or even Wydvil. On Elizabeth's tomb it is spelt Widville. Throughout this text the modern form of Woodville will be used.

1461

On 29 March John Grey tragically lost his life while leading the Lancastrian Cavalry of Henry VI into battle at Towton-Moor in Yorkshire during the Wars of the Roses. With this event, Elizabeth, his widow, and her two sons lost their Astley home and money, confiscated by the Yorkists. Elizabeth was forced to take her two sons and live with her parents at Grafton in Northamptonshire.

1464

(A3) During this year Elizabeth experienced a most dramatic reversal of fortunes following a story of very romantic developments. The twenty-seven-year-old Elizabeth heard that the Yorkist King Edward IV was going hunting in Whittlebury forest close to her home. She made for the forest and eventually threw herself in front of the King's horse, pleading for a hearing.

(B6) Elizabeth begged for the return of her Astley estates for her two sons. The King, who was really taken by her beauty, not only agreed to her plea but eventually proposed to her. The couple were married in secret during the early hours of 1 May, but the event was not made public until Edward paraded her through London months later.

It was the first instance of a British sovereign marrying a subject, but the occasion was not popular in all circles.

Elizabeth Woodville's large family were very unpopular with nobles and dignitaries and her marriage deeply offended the Earl of Warwick. Her son Thomas Grey, who married the King's niece, was created Marquess of Dorset.

1483

The death of King Edward IV sparked a terrific power struggle throughout England which appeared to lead to the deaths of the Princes in the Tower.

Although never proven, the Princes, both sons of Edward IV and Elizabeth Woodville, were supposedly murdered by Richard, Duke of Gloucester, who eventually succeeded his brother to become Richard III.

1485

The Wars of the Roses came to an end when Richard III lost his life and his crown to Henry VII on Bosworth field.

Tudor Period

1486

The Tudor period began with the marriage of Elizabeth of York to Henry VII; the new queen was also a product of Edward IV's marriage to Elizabeth Woodville. The wedding took place on 18 January.

1487

The potentially dangerous Woodvilles had much of their power reduced when Henry VII, the Dowager Queen Elizabeth's son-in-law, confiscated her seventy country estates. Deprived of the income from them, Elizabeth retired to the sanctuary of Bermondsey Abbey during February. The Abbey stood on the opposite side of the river Thames to the Tower of London.

1491

The future Henry VIII was born on 28 June, a grandson for Elizabeth Woodville.

1492

Elizabeth Woodville's controversial life came to an end when, surrounded by her daughters, she passed away at Bermondsey Abbey on 8 June. The one-time resident of Astley is remembered by two notable portraits: a wooden panel in King's College, Cambridge, a college she co-founded, and a stained-glass portrait in the Great North window of Canterbury Cathedral, part of a series of the family of King Edward IV.

1530

At the age of fifty-three, the second Marquis of Dorset, Sir Thomas Grey, died at Astley.

Sir Thomas was the grandson of Elizabeth Woodville and her first husband Sir John Grey, who was killed in battle in 1461.

The Marquis was succeeded by his son Henry, future Duke of Suffolk and father to Lady Jane Grey.

1535

Sebastian Newdegate, son of John and Amphilisia Newdegate, died a martyr's death, when he was hanged, drawn and quartered at Tyburn.

Originally Sebastian was a courtier of Henry VIII who became a monk. He died for refusing to acknowledge the King's supremacy. He was one of a very large family – ten sons and seven daughters.

1536

Erdbury Priory became one of the early casualties when Henry VIII dissolved the monasteries. Those with an annual return of less than £200 were the first to go, Erdbury was valued at £100.5s.5¼d. The 2002 equivalent value was £37,800.20.

1538

Erdbury, having been confiscated by the crown, was given with a multitude of lands to Charles Brandon, Duke of Suffolk, brother-in-law of King Henry VIII.

1539

The dissolution was complete with the closure of most of the larger monasteries.

1541

John Newdegate was born, later to become the family's first owner of Arbury Hall.

1545

The collegiate establishment at Astley came to an end.

Anne and John Newdegate, memorial brass, Harefield Church, 1545

The Duke of Suffolk, Sir Henry Grey,
father of Lady Jane and owner of Astley Castle

1551

Sir Henry Grey, the last of the Greys to own the Astley estates, became the Duke of Suffolk. Henry had married Frances, daughter of the previous Duke, Charles Brandon. To him and the Duchess three daughters were born, the ladies Jane, Catherine, and Mary.

1553

During the summer began an episode in history that again linked Astley with the throne of England.

The very fragile Edward VI, who had been induced to name 'Lady Jane Grey as his successor, died on the evening of 6 July, with four of the strongest and most fundamental values of the sixteenth century: religion, patriotism, due legal process and dynastic loyalty in conflict with each other.' As described by the powerful words of David Starkey.

The Dukes of Northumberland and Suffolk, Sir John Dudley and Sir Henry Grey, had influenced and supported the decision to proclaim the Protestant Lady Jane Grey as Queen at the Tower on 10 July. Meanwhile, the Catholic and legal claimant Mary, daughter of Henry VIII, challenged for the throne in East Anglia. Her standard was raised and as a Tudor she received tremendous support. Mary was proclaimed Queen at the Tower on 19 July.

Rival Jane Grey and her intended consort were honourably detained in the Tower, while her father Sir Henry Grey along with the Duke of Northumberland and fellow conspirators Sir John Gates and Sir Thomas Palmer were also imprisoned in the Tower. On 31 July, Sir Henry Grey was pardoned and released, while the Duke of Northumberland, along with Sir John Gates and Sir Thomas Palmer, was executed.

1554

(A10) Revolt was in the air early in the year, with a rebellion known as 'Wyatt's Revolt', when four different risings in the south and middle England, under the command of Thomas Wyatt of Kent, planned to overthrow the government and the Catholic Queen Mary, also ruining her plans to marry Philip of Spain. The plan was to march on London from four different parts of the compass. Wyatt's army would come from the south-east, while the Duke of Suffolk, Sir Henry Grey, would raise the Midland counties. The Carew family would raise an army in the south west, and Sir James Croft would appear from the Welsh marches.

The plot leaked, however, and Henry Grey fled to his country estate at Astley where he placed himself under the care of a gamekeeper named Underwood. Grey hid for three days and nights in a huge hollow oak tree, a remnant of the old forest of Arden, before he was betrayed by the keeper, who was tempted by a £200 'dead or alive' reward on Grey's head. He was captured by the Earl of Huntingdon and taken to the Tower, arriving under heavy guard in London on Saturday, 10 February, just two days before his unfortunate daughter Lady Jane Grey was beheaded on the Tower green. Her husband, (C8) Guildford Dudley, Northumberland's fourth son, was also executed. On 17 February, Grey was sentenced to death during a trial in Westminster Hall. A public execution followed on Tower Hill on Friday, 23 February. The Duke's widow Frances continued to live at Astley for a few more years and eventually married a member of her staff, Adrian Stokes. The marriage caused a great scandal.

1555

Astley castle was rebuilt in consequence of the Duke's treason. A remodelled castle was reduced to an ordinary house. All fortifications and outer defences were pulled down and demolished. It was during this period that Adrian Stokes, now residing at the castle, laid his hands on revenues belonging to the church. Not content with this, Stokes also stripped the lead from the very tall church spire, an act of vandalism that was to have severe consequences in later years.

Elizabethan Period

1559

First mention of a Manor House at Harefield.

1567

During the early years of Queen Elizabeth I's reign, a fashion was sweeping across England of wealthy people buying ruined monastic buildings and surrounding land, and converting them into grand manor houses.

And that's exactly what happened when a wealthy lawyer of Scottish descent, Sir Edmund Anderson, purchased the ruined Erdbury Priory and its vast estate from the heirs of the Duke of Suffolk.

1571

John Newdegate, the eldest son of the Middlesex MP of the same name, was born at Harefield. His mother was Newdegate's first wife, Martha Cave.

1575

Martha Cave died aged twenty-nine years.

1577

Sir Edmund Anderson impressed Queen Elizabeth I so much that he succeeded Sir James Dyer as Sergeant at Arms. Anderson, described as an early Judge Jeffries, was particularly severe with both Catholic and Protestant dissenters.

Queen Elizabeth I by John Bettes

1581

The rising Sir Edmund Anderson acquired Brackenhoe Manor, at Thurleigh in Bedfordshire.

1582

Anderson's rise continued when he was promoted to Lord Chief Justice of the Common Pleas.

1584

Anderson's Warwickshire home, Arbury Hall, was complete, built on the foundation of the former Augustinian Priory. It was quadrangular in shape, built around a central courtyard.

In Middlesex, John Newdegate senior was outlawed for his debts.

1585

Sir Edmund Anderson was finding it very difficult living at Arbury, far from his increasing judicial duties in London. The roads in Elizabethan England were appalling surfaces, rutted and boggy, lacking any kind of drainage, some stretches were completely impassable during winter or wet weather. And so Anderson sought a home nearer London.

With John Newdegate's financial problems mounting, the two gentlemen negotiated an exchange of properties.

Harefield was more valuable than the less attractive Arbury Hall, so John Newdegate received a balance of some £8,400 pounds – a princely sum in those days. The 2002 equivalent value was £1,478,000.

1586

In July the Newdegates took up residence at Arbury Hall.

Sir Edmund Anderson moved to Harefield before helping to frame the indictment against Mary Queen of Scots, along with Solicitor General Sir Thomas Egerton. They also sat at the trial of the fated Queen. Due to illness of the Speaker, Queen Elizabeth appointed Anderson Deputy Speaker.

John Newdegate exchanged Harefield Manor for Arbury Hall in 1586. Portrait by Ewart.

Sir Edmund Anderson, first owner of Arbury Hall
by English School

1587

(A12) On 27 February, Mary Queen of Scots was executed at Fotheringay Castle. Just a few weeks later, the arranged wedding took place between the sixteen-year-old John Newdegate and the tender twelve-year-old Ann Fitton, daughter of the wealthy and well-connected knight, Sir Edward Fitton. The fighting Fittons, as they were known, came from Gawsworth Hall in Cheshire.

(B7) The wedding took place on 30 April, and the bride's father, Sir Edward, undertook to pay, in addition to a small dowry, all John Newdegate senior's debts in all their unspecified entirety. In exchange John Newdegate generously settled the Arbury estates on the newlyweds, retaining for himself small parcels of land in Middlesex.

However, Sir Edward eventually discovered that John was responsible for debts far in excess of the amounts he envisaged. At some stage after this John Newdegate was admitted into Fleet debtors jail in London.

1588

Soon after acquiring Harefield, the wealthy Anderson purchased Stratton Manor from the Pygot family.

1592

During February Sir John Newdegate senior died in Fleet prison and was buried on the twenty-sixth day of the month.

Fleet debtors prison was notorious for cruelty to prisoners, particularly under the wardenship of Thomas Bainbridge in the eighteenth century.

It was demolished in 1846 from its position on the east side of Farringdon Street in London.

1594

Sir Edmund Anderson now became Lord of the Manor of Eyeworth in Bedfordshire, and alienated the manor house from Sir John Fortesque. This became the family seat from the following year.

1595

Young John Newdegate, now twenty-four years of age, finally took up residence in Arbury Hall. His sister-in-law, the beautiful and lively Mary Fitton, became a maid of honour to Queen Elizabeth. Mary immediately enchanted the elderly comptroller of the Queen's household, Sir William Knollys, but she was to cause him problems when her manner infected the other maids of honour.

1599

Will Kemp the famous clown dedicated his 'Nine days' wonder', a Morris dance from London to Norwich, to Ann Fitton.

1600

(A7) John and Ann continued to work hard at Arbury, and in view of his undoubted financial weakness and absence of local family roots, it seems remarkable that by this year his name was included on the Commission of the Peace. John was twenty-nine and although an outsider in Warwickshire society he did have friends in high places. His sister-in-law Mary Fitton was still one of the Queen's maids of honour, and other court connections included Sir Fulke Greville and the Paget and Knollys families.

(B8) The hardworking couple celebrated the birth of a son during this time whom they also called John.

(C3) As a result of Adrian Stokes' vandalism a few years earlier, disaster struck the church at Astley with the lofty spire crashing down in a storm, taking a large part of the church with it. Without the lead on the roof the weather had got in and caused catastrophic damage, which eventually led to the possession of the church and castle being conveyed to Sir Richard Chamberlayne.

The affluent Sir Edmund Anderson of Harefield was busy purchasing the site of the Manor of Monks Hardwick, the title of which at the time of the Dissolution was held by St Neot's Priory. Sir Edmund KE, Chief Justice of the Common Pleas, purchased the reversion and the moated site from Henry Cromwell. On it he appears to have built a large half-timbered house of which one wing survives to this day.

1601

(A3) Sir Edmund now sells Harefield Manor, former home of the Newdegate family, to Alice Countess of Derby and her second husband Sir Thomas Egerton, Lord Keeper of the Great Seal. Her first husband Ferdinando, the fifth Earl of Derby, was poisoned in 1594. The Dowager Countess was the youngest daughter of Sir John Spencer, ancestor of the Dukes of Marlborough, and so related to Sir Winston Churchill and the late Princess Diana.

(B7) It is interesting to note that the Newdegate possession of Harefield may have been broken for ninety years, but the family link was not completely severed, as Lord Egerton's only daughter was mother of Juliana, Lady Newdegate.

At the court of Elizabeth I, the beautiful but promiscuous Mary Fitton was dismissed following a whirlwind affair with the enamoured Earl of Pembroke. Mary went to live with her sister Ann at Arbury where she gave birth to a baby boy, who sadly survived only a few days. The Queen was very annoyed that another of her chaste young maids had proved frail, and rewarded the Earl with a few days in prison to cool off. Mary Fitton is believed by many to be the Dark Lady of Shakespeare's Sonnets.

1602

(A3) Lord Egerton and his wife Alice, Countess of Derby, were great favourites of Queen Elizabeth, and they entertained her lavishly for three days from 31 July to 2 August. It proved to be one of the most momentous occasions in the history of Harefield. The cost of the grand event to Lord Egerton was more than £4,000, even though his friends had supplied many gifts. Among the presents were seventy-four bucks, fifteen swans, 178 partridge, 200 prawns, twenty firkins of oysters, and forty boxes of fruits. The occasion was marred only by the weather, for it rained incessantly; St Swithen got the blame.

(B12) At Arbury, Ann and John Newdegate were gifted with the birth of a second son, who they were to name Richard.

Stuart Period

1603

(A7) With the death of Queen Elizabeth on 24 March, James I succeeded to the throne of England. The new king was to knight John Newdegate at Whitehall, a title that was paid for by Ann's great-uncle Francis Fitton, who was married to the Duchess of Northumberland. The honour in a way seemed to be some kind of reward for John's valiant efforts with his financial battle at Arbury.

Two of his projects failed miserably; a local coal mine was abandoned after about a year when returns proved meagre, and a loss of £250 was recorded in the ironworks at the Fitton's Cheshire seat at Gawsworth.

(B14) Harefield Manor's former owner Sir Edmund Anderson sat at the trial in Winchester of the fated Sir Walter Raleigh.

The former favourite of Queen Elizabeth was found guilty of treason during a trial described as a farce. Sir Edmund, Chief Justice of the Commons Pleas, sat as a judge alongside Sir John Popham, Chief Justice of the King's Bench.

(C3) The new owner of Harefield, Sir Thomas Egerton, was promoted to Lord Chancellor.

1605

(A14) Sir Edmund Anderson died on 1 August, aged seventy-five. He was laid to rest in the Church of All Saints at Eyeworth in Bedfordshire. The man who built Arbury Hall left a large fortune multiplying many times the £1,000 he inherited from his father.

He left a widow and six surviving children (his eldest son, Edmund, pre-deceased him).

(B23) The ornamental monument to Sir Edmund and his wife Magdalen (Smyth) consists of a fine marble altar tomb upon which are two recumbent effigies, one representing the former very successful Chief Justice in his judicial robes of office.

Mary Fitton, by the circle of George Gower

Sir John Newdegate, knighted in 1603, by English School

The resting place of Sir Edmund Anderson, All Saints Church, Eyeworth, Bedfordshire

The tomb of Sir Edmund Anderson

1606

The year ended on a sad note for Sir John Newdegate with the death of a friend – Sir Fulke Greville. The former servant of Queen Elizabeth and Councillor of King James I was buried at Warwick on 14 December.

1607

Sir Richard Chamberlayne of Astley started to restore the church, which had been partially destroyed by Adrian Stokes' vandalism. He pulled down the ruined chapel and transept, rebuilt the tower and with reclaimed materials from the ruin he built the chancel. It gave the church its present form.

1608

Sir Thomas Egerton built a new mansion house at Harefield.

1610

Sadly, our young knight Sir John Newdegate died at the tender age of thirty-nine.

Although he was succeeded by his son of the same name, the fact that the boy was just ten years old meant that his mother Ann kept things going at Arbury. Sir John was buried at Harefield on 10 April, and remembered by a very elaborate coloured and gilded monument in the Brackenbury Chapel.

1617

Sir Thomas Egerton died shortly after being made Baron Ellesmere and Viscount Brackley.

1618

Ann Fitton, now in her mid-forties, died, and at Arbury the estate had devolved on to the third successive John. He went on to marry Susanna Luls, the daughter of a wealthy Dutch merchant, Arnold Luls.

John's brother Richard went to Trinity College, Oxford to continue his education.

1620

Richard left Oxford and eventually started his legal training at Greys Inn, at the age of eighteen.

1628

Richard Newdigate, the first of the family to spell the name with an 'i', was called to the Bar to begin what turned out to be a very lucrative career.

1632

During February at the Church of St Bartholomew, Great Smithfield, the twenty-nine-year-old Richard Newdigate married Juliana, the twenty-one-year-old daughter of Sir Francis Leigh of Newnham Regis, Warwickshire Knight of the Bath, and granddaughter of the late Baron Ellesmere, Sir Thomas Egerton. The couple settled at Leaden Porch, Holborn, where eight of their eleven children were born.

1637

Alice, Countess of Derby, died at Harefield on 26 January, and the estate passed to her eldest daughter by the Earl of Derby, the first husband of Lady Ann.

Her magnificent monument by Maximillian Colt enhances the south-east corner of the chancel in Harefield church. He carved monuments to many famous people, including that of Elizabeth I in Westminster.

1642

The Surrey branch of the Newdigate family became extinct. Arbury Hall also changed hands when John Newdigate died, bringing to an end the period of three successive Johns. His marriage to Susanna Luls passed without issue (though one boy was born, he sadly died during infancy). And so Arbury passed to John's brother Richard in a year that saw England in turmoil, with the outbreak of civil war. In fact the first major battle took place just a few miles away at Edge Hill in the south of the county.

St Mary the Virgin, Astley, restored in 1607

Almshouses, Harefield, bequeathed by the Countess of Derby

1642–43

During the civil war Richard Newdigate was sympathetic to the parliamentarian cause, for during this period he held the position of Lieutenant of Horse for their army.

1644

The eagerly and long-awaited heir to Richard arrived on 5 May, when Juliana gave birth to their eighth child and first surviving son. The boy was named Richard after his father.

1646

There appears to have been a civil war skirmish at Astley, for the great Warwickshire historian Dugdale records that, on 16 January, 'Astley House in Warrshire surprised by my Lord of Loughborough's forces the Governour (a shoemaker) and the rest in the house prisoners and carried away with most of the armies, ammunition etc.'

So it seems that the house which was still the seat of the Chamberlaynes had been occupied by parliamentarians and this extract refers to the recapture by Royalist troops.

1648

Richard was Commissioner for the Militia (raising troops) for Middlesex.

1649

(A12) Richard senior was appointed Justice of the Peace for the county, though never attended Quarter sessions.

(B3) At Harefield Church the incumbent was Mr Hoare, placed there by Parliament.

1654

(A12) The legal career of Richard Newdigate senior took another step forward when he was made a Sergeant-at-Law under

Cromwell. This is a position normally conferred by the crown. During this year he was also appointed a Justice of the Upper Bench.

(B8) Sir Richard Chamberlayne passed away at Astley and the man who had restored the church earlier in the century was buried on 6 November in the chancel of St Mary the Virgin.

1655

(A3) Harefield, which had passed through Anne, daughter of Alice, Countess of Derby, was now owned by her son George. He in turn passed the estate to his widow Jane, who then married Sir William Sedley Bart.

(B12) Sir Richard Newdigate (who will now be referred to as Sergeant) continued to live near his legal heartland in London, visiting Arbury only during the summer recess. He was committed to York to preside over the trial connected to the rebellion known as the Penruddock Rising, when a group of royalists including John Baron Belayse (member of the Sealed Knot and leader of the Northern Royalists) along with the Earl of Dumfries and Colonel James Halsey were indicted on a charge of treason.

It proved to be a rather momentous occasion in the Sergeant's life, for when bravely instructing the jury to acquit his fellow lords, he declared he knew no law that made it high treason to levy war against a Lord Protector.

Oliver Cromwell was not unnaturally displeased and put the Judge out of office.

This was a law defined in the statute of Edward III, which meant that without a monarch there could be no treason.

1657

Back in favour, the Sergeant was reinstated on the bench.

1658

Shortly after Cromwell's death on 3 September, Sergeant rose to be Chief Justice under the returned Rump Parliament, and though appointed Sergeant-at-Law, never held any further office.

Sir Richard Newdigate, first Baronet, by Zoust

1660

(A15) Charles II was restored to the throne in May, but, about four months on, the Sergeant relinquished his position. Due to a conflict of stories one cannot be certain whether he was dismissed or resigned; however, the move avoided the possibility of embarrassment after holding high office under Cromwell. Sergeant returned to his own legal practice.

(B3) During the same year disaster struck Harefield when a fire completely destroyed most of the habitable parts of the manor, now owned by George Pitt of Strathfieldsday, who had become the third husband of Jane, granddaughter of the Duchess of Derby.

The only surviving parts of Harefield Place were the two lodges, one at each end of the building. Apparently the blame for the fire fell on a guest, Sir Charles Sedley, who was reading in bed by candlelight.

1661

At the age of seventeen, the Sergeant's son Richard was being educated at Christchurch College, Oxford.

1665

(A12) Young Richard reached the age of twenty-one in May and it turned out to be quite a momentous year for him. Just six months later his father settled on him most of his Warwickshire lands, and so in November Richard began making plans to live at Arbury Hall.

(B15) Just three weeks later, on 21 December, he married Mary Bagot, one of five daughters of Sir Edward Bagot, second Baronet of Blithefield Hall in Staffordshire.

Mary also had twelve brothers. It was an arranged marriage, just like his parents' and grandparents' had been.

1666

Richard and Mary moved permanently to live at Arbury – the beginning of a forty-four-year period that began shaping the Arbury Hall we know today.

Work continued with the planting of Norway firs along North Walk, an idea obviously started several years earlier, and eventually the Avenue, extended from the Hall right through to North Lodge. (At the time known as North Firs.)

The first child was born on 10 December when Mary gave birth to a son. He was named John after Richard's grandfather, and present at his christening, held on Richard and Mary's first wedding anniversary, were godparents Sergeant and Juliet Newdigate and the Archbishop of Canterbury, Gilbert Sheldon. Sadly, John died in infancy.

This began a period of nineteen years of childbearing during which time Mary produced fifteen children, eight boys and seven girls, of which eleven reached adulthood – a good rate at that time.

1668

(A12) On 29 April, a second child was born. Named Richard, he became known as Dick and provided the family with an heir. An account survives from Christmas of this year and rather interestingly lists food and drink consumed by the household over a twelve-day period. A list of presents precedes it: (B15)

> 6 veal, 1 quarter mutton, 5 turkeys, 44 geese, 55 capons, 48 pullets, 1 pay bird, 3 pigs, 200 eggs, 86 pounds of butter, 38 chickens, 10 sugar loaves, 12 cakes, 2 barrels of oysters.

> Spent by the Cook:
> 2 beefs, 6 muttons, 6 veal, 18 turkeys, 50 geese, 16 ducks, 42 capons, 2 pullets, 32 chickens, 3 pigs, 1 swan, 1 pay bird, 100 couples of rabbits, 10 strikes of wheat.

> Spent by the Baker:
> 5 strikes of wheat, 6 strikes of blendcorn, 17½ strikes of millcorn.

> Spent by the Dairymaid:
> 140 pounds of butter.

> Spent by the Housekeeper:
> 17 hogsheads of beer, 3 hogsheads of ale, one barrel of march beer.

It is known that Richard operated with a large household of servants, which at one stage stood as high as twenty-eight.

1670

With Richard now settled at Arbury, his parents began looking at the possibility of repurchasing the old family home of Harefield Place in Middlesex.

Although reduced by the fire ten years earlier, it clearly had its attractions as a place of family pride, and a country home near London, that could be used in retirement by Sergeant and Julian. The property was also still owned by Mr George Pitts, a distant relative of Julian.

1674

So lucrative had Sergeant's legal practice become that he was able to make two major purchases for the family. First he bought Astley Castle and its lands from the then representatives of the Chamberlayne family. And in November he announced that after four years of negotiation with the suspicious Mr Pitts he had repurchased the family home of almost ninety years ago, Harefield Place.

This meant that from this time the Newdigates were proudly in possession of all three Manors.

At Arbury, Sir William Wilson and Sir Christopher Wren were becoming involved in Richard's grand ideas for lavish new stables for his horses. The two architects submitting drawings for a porch to fit the plan.

1675

Work began on 9 February to dig out the foundations for the stable block, which lay along the course of an old moat. Stone bought in from Attleborough quarries proved eight feet deep in places along the footing, while above ground the building was of brick with stone coigns and facings.

The bricks were made at Adam Broughton's yard adjoining Arbury Park.

Taking into account the religious background of Richard, and with an ever-growing family, it is no surprise that at this time work was also moving towards forming a private family chapel in the north east corner of the house. This decision must have been influenced by the repeated christenings and churching plus the children's religious education.

1676

There were known to be 210 recorded inhabitants living at Astley.

1677

Seventeen years after the Restoration, Sergeant received some well-deserved recognition for his brave service to royalists back in 1655. Lord Halsey, who owed his life to Sergeant's action, initiated the proceedings and was greatly supported by two of Newdigate's friends, Lord Armorer and Lord Grandison, who reminded King Charles of the events at York Assizes. The King thanked him for his kindness to royalists 'in the worst of times', and rewarded him with a Baronetcy. It was hoped that the Sergeant would be reinstated as Chief Justice, but on 24 July he was happy to be created Sir Richard Newdigate, Baronet. It was at this time normal to pay £1,000 for the title, but on this occasion the fee was waived.

1678

Sir Richard sadly enjoyed his title for only fifteen months, as he died on 14 October. The honour could only pass down through the male line of the family and his son Richard at Arbury Hall duly became the second Baronet.

Work on the new chapel and stables was well advanced, and the involvement of Sir Christopher Wren and carver Grinling Gibbons has been mentioned but cannot be proven. One thing that is certain is that City of London plasterer Edward Martin executed the magnificent Caroline Fretwork ceiling in the chapel for a sum of £39. Both ventures were nearing completion. Legend has it that family friend the Archbishop of Canterbury, Gilbert

Archbishop of Canterbury Gilbert Sheldon
consecrated Arbury Chapel in 1677

Arbury stables.
The entrance porch was designed by Sir Christopher Wren in 1678.

Sheldon, consecrated the chapel. Sheldon was an advisor to Charles II. However it is known that Wren, who was busy working on St Paul's at the time, did submit two designs for the stable porch for which Sir Richard presented him with a pair of silver candlesticks worth £11.9s when they met at Oxford. The Baronet also paid architect Sir William Wilson £1 for a similar drawing. It is not certain whose design we see today, though the experts favour Wren's design.

1680

Astley Castle was now being used by the ever-growing family, and not only was it home to the Baronet's agent, Mr Christopher Merry, but also to family tutor Mr Wyat and four of Sir Richard's children. The boys boarding at Astley were Dick, the heir to the estate, and brothers Walter, John and Gilbert.

1681

Sir Richard began the great survey of Chilvers Coton. The parish and manor was originally one Lordship divided into three estates during the twelfth and thirteenth centuries. This survey eventually filled five volumes and took account of virtually everyone and everything in the area. The project took several years to complete.

1683

On Sunday, 1 July a search for arms took place at Arbury in connection with the recently failed Rye House plot. Around 10 a.m. Sir Richard was disturbed during prayer in the family chapel by the High Sheriff of Warwickshire, Captain Lucy and a party of horsemen.

Rumour had it that the Baronet was secretly holding a consignment of arms, but the only weapons found were Sir Richard's own rather ill-kept armoury of which he was obviously embarrassed. Nine suits of armour and fourteen pairs of pistols were confiscated along with a drum which was duly returned at a later date, when it was realised that its use in Arbury was as a dinner gong. Captain Lucy apologised to the Baronet for the inconvenience.

1684

The Baronet's local mining operations continued to struggle and lose money with flooding becoming a major problem. A joint venture with adjoining landowner Thomas Coventry was set up to extract coal from Nuneaton Common.

The first volume of the *Great Survey of Chilvers Coton* was completed in July, and a further two by the end of the year.

1685

Juliana, widow of the Sergeant, died on 9 December; she had survived her husband by seven years.

1689

Early in the year Sir Richard became involved with the Birmingham Gunsmiths, which eventually led to him becoming a founder member of the Birmingham Small Arms company (BSA as it was later known).

The failed joint mining operations of the Baronet and Thomas Coventry had ceased to exist. Coal pits were leased to Thomas Ludford of Ansley Hall and Theodore Stratford of Atherstone for a period of ten years.

1691

Head gardener at Arbury was Jo Dagley. This was a time when gardening had become very fashionable all over the country, inspired by the interest shown by Queen Mary since William's accession to the throne in 1688. Sir Richard had always been enthusiastic though, and dealt with highly reputable firms as London and Wise for his seeds and young trees. He grew a wide range of plants including orange and lemon trees. Gardeners employed at Arbury during this period earned eight pence a day for a man, and four pence for a woman.

1692

On 14 September, Mary Bagot, first wife of the second Baronet, died aged forty-eight. Mary had presented Sir Richard with no fewer than fifteen children during their marriage, eight boys and seven girls.

She was buried at Harefield on 19 September, and is remembered by a huge monument on the north side of the altar in the chancel, carved by that celebrated carver Grinling Gibbons.

Amphillis, the eldest daughter, took on the role of mistress.

1694

Making their home at Astley Castle were newlyweds Dick and Sarah. Dick was the heir to Sir Richard, and Sarah Bishop daughter of the Baronet Cecil Bishop of Parham in Sussex.

1695

Dick's marriage ended prematurely when Sarah, his wife of just fifteen months, died in childbirth.

Sir Richard's enthusiasm for his horses was reflected in the variety and quality being stabled at Arbury at this time. Every type, including hunters, Arabs and brood mares, were housed in his elaborate building.

A total of sixty-seven horses were kept, along with two small packs of hounds for hunting fox and buck.

1699

Following the peace treaty of Ryeswick two years earlier between Louis XIV and William III, the Baronet became interested in a tour of France to see for himself what state the country was in. Taking his own coach he departed Harefield on 30 June, along with his son Dick and seventeen-year-old daughter Betty. Three of his household staff from Arbury made up the party: Francis Coles, the housekeeper, Harry Haines, the coachman, and Jack Royl, his postillion. The small group sailed first to Cowes on the Isle of Wight, before sailing to Cherbourg by 15 July. The tour through France was, to say the least, uncomfortable, and a lot of hardship was suffered. The route lay through Caen, Evreux, and St Germaine to Paris, where a week was spent in the capital. Then on via Beauvais to Bologna, and finally Calais. The party was no doubt relieved to land at Dover on 11 August. This proved to be anything other than a grand tour.

1703

The fifty-nine-year-old Sir Richard Newdigate married his second wife, the young Henrietta Wiggington of Hams in Surrey, at Arbury on 6 August.

1704

Also finding a new bride was Dick, the heir to Arbury, who married Elizabeth Twisden, daughter of Sir Roger Twisden, Baronet of Bradbourne in Kent. Dick and Elizabeth started their new life in the parish of St Martin in the Fields, London. The fact that he settled far away from his previous home at Astley was down to the deep rift between him and his father over the Baronet's ongoing extravagant lifestyle and the possibility of inheriting massive debt.

Meanwhile at Arbury Sir Richard and Henrietta suffered the experience of a stillborn child.

It is believed Henrietta eventually bore three children, but there is no record of any surviving infancy.

1710

On 4 January, the Baronet's life came to an end when he died in his sixty-sixth year. He was survived by nine of the twelve children that had outlived infancy.

During his life nothing but the best would do, and products of his policy are very much enjoyed today nearly three hundred years later. The elaborate stable building, family chapel, beautiful portraits by the renowned Dutch-born court painter Sir Peter Lely, all remain as monuments of quality to the lavish lifetime of Sir Richard Newdigate, second Baronet.

He was buried along with first wife Lady Newdigate (Mary Bagot), on Friday, 13 January at Harefield Church.

So the estates of Arbury, Astley and Harefield devolved to the forty-two-year-old Dick, who became Sir Richard Newdigate, third Baronet.

Old Arbury Hall by Henry Beighton, 1708

1711

At this time there were four coal pits on the Baronet's land.

1712

Dick and his wife Elizabeth finally settled to live at Arbury. By this time Lady Newdigate had produced six children, of which only three daughters lived to maturity.

Georgian Period

1715

Dick, the third Baronet, and Elizabeth, Lady Newdigate, produced their fourth son Edward; he was their eighth child.

1719

The seventh son and youngest of eleven children was born on 31 May to the Baronet and Lady Newdigate. He was named Roger and destined to become one of the most famous names in Newdigate family history.

There were very few major changes during the third Baronet's time at Arbury; maybe this was because of the debts he had inherited from his extravagant father.

What does survive today, however, are the beautiful wrought-iron gates, erected and made by the Nottingham firm of Francis Foljambe, by the stables at the entrance to the gardens. It's perhaps just a coincidence that these handsome gates were commissioned at the time of Sir Roger's birth.

1727

Sir Richard Newdigate, the third Baronet, died aged fifty-nine, after a fairly short term of seventeen years as head of the family. His wife Elizabeth had him laid to rest at Harefield Church and commissioned Michael Rysbrach, one of the leading sculptors of the day, to make a bust of him.

The family estate now settled on the tender young shoulders of the eleven-year-old Edward. He was one of only three surviving boys, the others being Richard and Roger, and became the fourth Baronet.

1730

The struggling family coal mine at Griff was closed.

1732

Sir Edward lost another of his brothers when Richard died of smallpox. This sad event meant he now had just one brother, Roger, and three sisters, Elizabeth, Mary and Juliana, surviving from the original family of eleven.

1734

Sir Edward's own short life came to an end when he died of lingering consumption at the age of eighteen.

So at the tender age of fourteen, Sir Roger faced the prospect of inheriting the vast estates, being the seventh and only surviving son of the third Baronet. He was in education at Westminster School at the time.

1736

Sir Roger Newdigate, the fifth Baronet, matriculated to University College, Oxford to continue his education.

1738

Just a short time after coming down from university as a graduating Master of Arts, the Baronet embarked on the first of two continental tours.

The experience of the tour, which lasted just over two years, proved to be one long learning curve, and for the Baronet the perfect way to continue his education and perfect his social skills for the challenges that lay ahead.

Landing at Calais in August, Sir Roger was immediately impressed with the cleanliness and neatness of the French port, before continuing to Paris via Amiens and Chantilly. He stayed a week in the capital before travelling on to Angers, where he spent the following nine months brushing up on the French language and social arts.

1739

Sir Roger worked hard on his course in Angers, which ended in June. He then continued his leisurely route to southern France through La Rochelle, Bordeaux and Toulouse before turning east to Montpellier, Nimes and Marseilles. Six months was then spent touring the south of the country.

1740

By sea now the Baronet travelled to Leghorn, and made his passage overland to Pisa, Florence and Rome. Obviously inspired with architectural and historic interest, Sir Roger stayed four months making sketches and even taking lessons in architectural drawing from a local master. By May the tour continued north, gradually turning for home via Venice, Lyon, Versailles, Brussels and Amsterdam. He disembarked in London on 25 September. The tour had proved to be both educational and inspirational, firing the Baronet's imagination and whetting his appetite for classical literature.

During his absence Sir Roger had also reached the age of maturity, and with it came his inheritance of the family estates.

1742

On 5 August, the Baronet's political career began when he was duly elected to Parliament as Knight of the Shires of Middlesex.

1743

In May, Sir Roger Newdigate, fifth Baronet, married Sophia Conyers, daughter of Edward Conyers of Copt Hall, Essex and the Hon. Matilda Fermor, a daughter of Lord Leominster.

The death of Henry Beighton occurred. Beighton was a well-known local cartographer whose drawing of Arbury Hall during the time of Sir Richard, the third Baronet, in 1708, stands as a reminder of the way the Hall appeared before its eighteenth century transformation. Beighton was buried in the churchyard at Chilvers Coton.

Sir Richard Newdigate, third Baronet, by Dahl

Sir Edward Newdigate, fourth Baronet, by Peter Lens

1745

The Free School was built in Coton for the poor of the parish; it was founded by Lady Newdigate, Elizabeth Twisden, the Baronet's mother.

There were facilities for thirty poor boys and twenty poor girls. Everything, including clothes for the poorest, was funded by Sir Roger both in his lifetime and afterwards by a will.

1747

At the parliamentary election in July Sir Roger lost his seat for Middlesex, coming third in a four-cornered contest.

1749

Although Sir Roger was a frequent visitor to Harefield, his thoughts were set on making Arbury Hall in Warwickshire his family seat. He began making disposals of land to George Cook, who considerably increased his holding, known as Harefield Park.

1750

This particular year was in many ways a turning point for the thirty-one-year-old Baronet as he began the transformation of his Elizabethan house to one of early Gothic revival. He obtained the services of the gentleman architect, Sanderson Miller of Radway Grange in Warwickshire, to install a Gothic bow window to the library on the south-west corner of the Hall.

In the autumn Sir Roger was alerted to the possibility of resuming his political career as a candidate for Oxford University.

1751

The Baronet duly regained a parliamentary seat when he won handsomely at the elections in January.

1752

(A3) More disposals to George Cook followed when Sir Roger

sold some old mills on the river Coln. Two mills along this part of the river were mentioned in the *Domesday Book*.

(B17) At this time the Baronet's mother, Elizabeth Twisden, was known to be resident at Astley Castle. Repairs to the castle were made and the stable block was gothicised.

1756

The library was completed internally with plasterwork by Robert Moore and woodwork executed by Benjamin King. Sir Roger's relationship with Sanderson Miller ended with a disagreement over politics.

1758

The Baronet always took an interest in local matters and was made Captain of the Warwickshire Militia in December.

1760

(A3) The disposals at Harefield continued with the sale of Harefield Place and its grounds to John Truesdale.

(B17) Sir Roger was also busy trying to increase his holding of Warwickshire land by a substantial 378 acres of Chilvers Coton from his neighbour Lord Coventry.

1761

A new road from Griff to Arbury Hall was laid during the year. It was the first of several roads laid during Sir Roger Newdigate's lifetime which have survived in use right up to the present day.

1762

Work on the Gothic transformation of Arbury Hall continued, with the completion of the drawing room in the south-east corner of the building. Miller had been replaced by architect Henry Keene, surveyor to Westminster, who supplied Sir Roger with detailed drawings of monuments in the Abbey.

From an eighteenth-century engraving of Harefield Manor

Lady Newdigate, Elizabeth Twisden,
mother of Sir Roger Newdigate, fifth Baronet.
Pastel by George Knapton.

1764

Between April and June the family chapel at Arbury was refurbished; this included the laying of a new floor.

Richard Hayward, a Warwickshire-born sculptor, executed the fine parlour chimneypiece, which is a copy of Aymer de Vallence's fourteenth-century tomb in Westminster. It has an English centre plaque.

Work was well advanced on the enclosure of Chilvers Coton, while the cutting of the Coton Lawn canal had also began.

1765

(A15) Sir Roger's mother Elizabeth, the Dowager Lady Newdigate, died at Astley.

A beautifully embroidered Gothic-style Chippendale suite by Lady Newdigate still graces the hall to this day. A beautiful embroidered fire screen was worked during her final year, when she was eighty-four.

(B17) Although money had been spent on the castle during its use as a Dower house, the years following saw the building fall into disrepair. Around this time the multi-talented Baronet began work on digging his own canal system. Seaswood Pool was dammed and turned into a twenty-one acre header pool, to fuel a network of five-and-a-half miles of private inland waterways. His ambition was to supply the lucrative markets of Coventry, Banbury and Oxford with coal mined on his ever-extending Warwickshire estates.

1766

The new tenant of Astley Castle was Sir John Astley.

1768

Extensive alteration and restoration was carried out to the chancel of Harefield Church, when the architect Henry Keene, on the request of Sir Roger Newdigate, put in the present Gothic plaster ceiling. The chancel arch was also enlarged and a new east window was installed.

1769

This period was probably the busiest in the political life of the Baronet, with growing support for the Prime Minister, Lord North.

He also worked tirelessly on his canal interests lobbying both business and landed interests, raising the necessary finance to ensure legislation went through for the construction of the Coventry and Oxford canals.

1770

(A17) Travel by coach in the eighteenth century was still a dangerous, uncomfortable and dirty experience, and Sir Roger was known not to care for it very much. However it was something he, as a public figure, had to endure quite often. One such trip was made in record time.

As a matter of some urgency the Baronet was requested to meet with Lord North, the Prime Minister, as soon as possible in January. Leaving Arbury by coach at 3.30 a.m., he made Towcester and had breakfast by 10 a.m. Later he dined at St Albans before finally reaching the House of Commons at 7.30 p.m.

Sir Roger was very pleased with the time of sixteen hours for the hundred-mile journey. Normally this trip was spread over two days in each direction, on the southbound leg he would stay overnight at Dunstable or St Albans, and on the home run either at Dunstable or Daventry.

It was at this time, under the direction of Henry Keene, that work began on the conversion of the Elizabethan Great Hall into a dining room. This project was to complete the transformation of the south front at Arbury. The external work was completed with grey sandstone from the local quarries at Attleborough and Wilnecote.

(B18) The cutting of the Coton Lawn canal was now complete; it had taken six years. Another new coaching route was opened, today known as Harefield Lane.

1771

Griff Lodge was built.

1772

Round Tower Farm was built, and its tower is still a local landmark to this day.

1773

By now, plans known as the New Foundation were well advanced to open new collieries at Griff.

1774

(A15) Sir Roger Newdigate was returned as MP for Oxford University for a fifth and final term. However the Baronet was struck with great sadness on 8 July with the death of his much-loved wife Sophia.

Lady Newdigate had endured a long period of illness, and her death came as a great shock to Sir Roger. Sophia Conyers had been a very talented lady, and some of her embroidered furniture and wonderfully painted books of watercolours are still to be enjoyed at Arbury today.

(B17) Almost immediately, Sir Roger made plans for his second grand tour. Within a week he left for London with his companions – sister-in-law Mary Conyers and protégé Charles Parker. By the end of July the party were in France and eventually reached Florence, Naples and Rome. The trip was to last eighteen months, and, while it was based on pleasure, the Baronet's love of archaeology and visiting classical ruins were always top priority. Objects of art were also purchased and sent back to England to decorate his ever-changing Warwickshire home.

He also purchased a pair of ancient candelabra from Piranasi as a gift to Oxford University, which were eventually installed in the Radcliffe Library.

In Italy in particular Sir Roger made many sketches of ancient ruins, something he engaged in on his first tour, which appeared to stimulate his romantic Gothic design of Arbury.

The first waterborne delivery of coal was made from Griff to Coventry.

1776

On New Year's Day the group returned to London, and it was not long before the Baronet was involved in a whirlwind courtship with a new lady in his life, Hester Margaretta Mundy. After a few short months the couple were married at St Martin in the Fields, London. The bride was the thirty-nine-year-old daughter of Edward Mundy of Allstree and Shipley in Derbyshire.

Architect Henry Keene died with his dining rooms project far from complete. He was insolvent – having been paid £500 for workmen's wages, he paid out only £180. Keene was replaced by Henry Couchman of Warwick, who had been clerk of the works at Packington Hall.

1778

The Seaswood Canal was complete.

1779

The magnificent south façade, with its very elaborate stone carvings of the perpendicular style, reached completion along with the remodelling of the centrally situated Great Hall into a dining room. The superb dining hall boasts a wonderful cathedral-style fan-vaulted ceiling, very similar to that of Gloucester Cathedral. Relics of ancient Italy along with classical statues collected on the 1775 grand tour adorn the walls. The stone chimneypiece of the original hall was moved into the first floor gallery, to be replaced with a delicately carved one of oak in the Gothic taste.

The Tea House, known affectionately as the Umbrella House, was converted into a house on the east side of the building.

1780

(A17) After a successful career spanning almost thirty years as MP for Oxford University, Sir Roger Newdigate decided to stand down and retire from public life. His place in the summer parliamentary elections was taken by Sir William Dolben.

(B3) John Truesdale sold Harefield Place to William Baynes after twenty years.

Sophia Conyers, first wife of Sir Roger Newdigate,
by William Hoare

Hester Margaretta Munday, second wife of Sir Roger Newdigate,
by George Romney

1781

The proud owner of Arbury could now spend more time enjoying his Warwickshire estates and developing his numerous projects. He gained immense pleasure from walking in the park and discussing with his workmen every aspect of his interests. During this year a new road across the head of Seaswood Pool was developed. It is now part of the B4102, known as Astley Lane.

1782

The foundations of two new lodges, today known as the Round Towers, were dug on 14 September at a place called North Firs.

This imposing gatehouse to Arbury, which is still very much a local feature today was completed the following year.

A coppice of fir trees was cut down on completion of the building.

Another new road was completed when a route across the head of Seaswood Pool was developed, now part of the B4102 link with Astley village.

1783

(A18) Work took place to improve the estate road to Astley, while progress continued on the transformation of Arbury.

With the south front now complete on the Hall alterations, attention turned to the east wing. A fan-vaulted cloister, aptly named the Cloisters, was built to provide a corridor to serve all the rooms along that side, to link the new Arbury Hall with its monastic origins. In the first half of this decade it appears that along with the cloister Gothic embellishments were also added to the school room and little sitting room.

(B3) Domenico Motta, a music tutor from Italy, took up residence at Arbury by appointment of Hester Lady Newdigate. Sir Roger's second wife and her young protégé Miss Sally Shilton were avid musicians.

1784

With the Round Towers archway completed, North Walk was

extended to join with Swan Lane and Arley Street. Today these roads are known as Arbury Road and Ansley Road.

During the year Seaswood Pool Lock gates were also completed to control the flow of water into the canal system.

At Astley a third gatehouse was to be built known as Astley Lodge.

Sir Roger Newdigate purchased continental glass for the cloisters from James Broden and Sons, part of which is a sundial engraved with the date 1733, and is now listed with the British Sundial Society.

1785

Henry Couchman produced drawings for the Baronet from Westminster in preparation for the decoration of the lofty saloon. The sketches cost five guineas. Cloisters completed.

Astley Lodge was completed.

1786

(A18) Sir Roger still had land interest in Harefield, and decided to have a new lodge built there as his Middlesex residence. The foundation stone was laid on 11 April at a location three miles south of the church along the road to Uxbridge.

(B15) At Arbury, work commenced on the saloon, which was to have the most amazing plasterwork ceiling, inspired by the Henry VII Chapel in the Abbey of Westminster.

(C18) The year had started with the stone chimney piece from the new dining room being re-sited in the first floor gallery during January. It had enhanced the room previously used as the Elizabethan Great Hall since the days of Sir John and Ann Newdegate. In February the stairs to the Long Gallery were finished with the laying of the final stone steps.

1787

(A15) Arbury's own private canal system, boasting thirteen locks, two boat houses and almost six miles of waterways, was nearing completion. It was one of the most extensive private canals in the country.

The Round Towers Gatehouse, completed in 1783

Astley Gatehouse, 1785

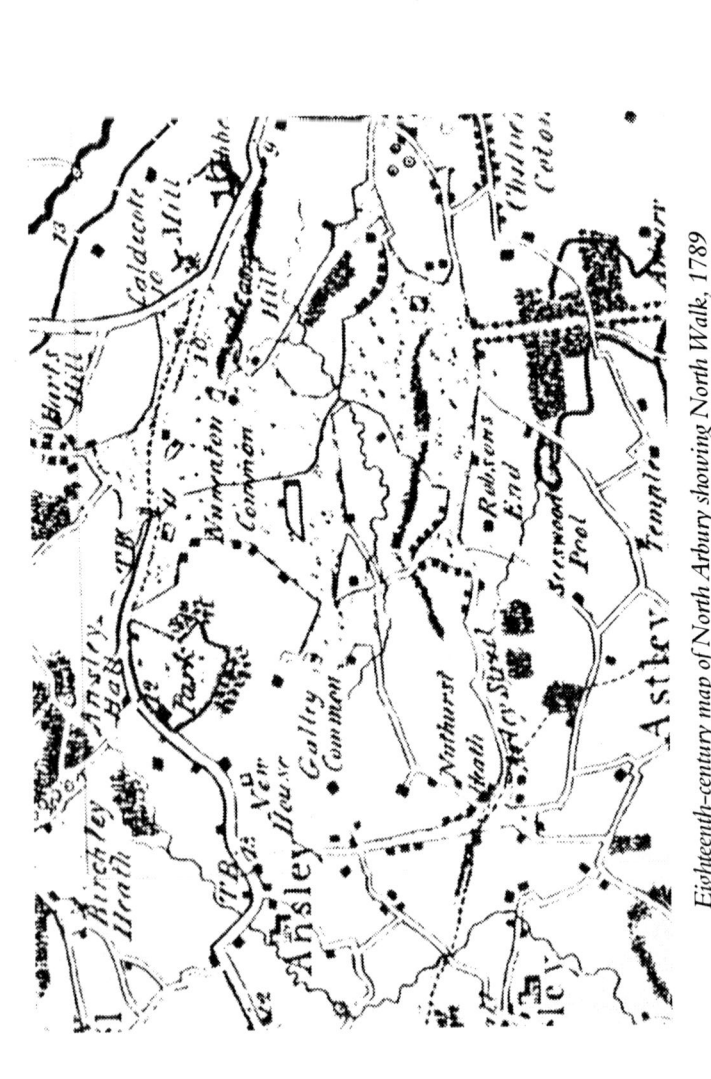

Eighteenth-century map of North Arbury showing North Walk, 1789

A new route to the Hall was also taking shape with the building of Somerlands Bridge, allowing coaches to sweep off North Walk by the Avenue before negotiating the canal bridge. This remains Arbury's main entrance to this day.

(B8) Mary Congers, Sir Roger's sister-in-law from his first marriage, was now resident at Astley Castle.

(C3) Charles Parker, Sir Roger's heir and protégé, took up residence at the new lodge in Harefield.

1790

The final section of the Coventry Canal was opened on 13 July, making it possible for the Baronet's Griff coal to be waterborne as far as Banbury.

1791

The death at Arbury of tutor Domenico Motta caused much sadness. The Italian had become very well liked by the family and established himself as a good friend.

1792–93

A cold bath house was being built at the side of North Walk, and by May it was up to floor level. The project was fully operational by June 1793. It was built over a natural spring, and such waters were considered very therapeutic. The building consisted of a bathing area at one end, and a dressing room at the southern end. Today it stands as a kind of stone monument to the past, and is wrongly believed by many visitors to be an old icehouse.

1795

(A17) Social unrest had been a problem for years since the food riots of 1756, and in April disturbances in Coventry, Nuneaton and Atherstone alarmed the Baronet so much that he armed his servants with bayonets to deter rioters coming from Astley.

(B15) The sudden death of Sir Roger's cousin and protégé Mr Charles Parker caused great sadness. Mr Parker was being groomed as a successor at Arbury because the Baronet had no

Sir Roger Newdigate's bath house, 1793

Somerlands Bridge, North Walk, Arbury

direct heirs of his own. Now in his seventy-sixth year he needed to make new arrangements. Charles Parker had been a tenant of Harefield Lodge.

At Arbury there was only one word to describe the completed saloon – magnificent. The room was enhanced by a beautiful projecting bay window with filigree tracery and tinted glass. The richly plastered ceiling by the little-known W Hanwell is a joy, and the walls are adorned by more than twenty Scagliola columns. The Baronet dedicated the saloon as a music room to his wife Hester, and their full-length portraits by George Romney remind us to this day.

Sadly, Lady Newdigate's health was deteriorating and she often escaped for relief to spa towns like Buxton, Cheltenham and Bognor.

The completion of a series of locks finally linked all three canals – Coventry, Oxford and Arbury's private waterway – together. By the end of the century, transportation of coal on these canals added £4,000 per year to the estate revenues.

1797

During November, Mary Conyers, resident of Astley Castle, died. The former sister-in-law of the Baronet, affectionately known as Molly, was laid to rest at Astley.

It was thought that Francis Parker of Wootton in Derbyshire, a brother of the late Charles Parker, would take up residence at the castle, for he often acted as Sir Roger's amanuensis in his later years. However, this did not materialise.

1800

Lady Hester Newdigate died on 30 September after suffering a long and painful illness. The second wife of the Baronet was buried at St Mary's Church, Harefield.

Work funded by Sir Roger began on the building of a college for the poor at Chilvers Coton. French prisoners from the Napoleonic wars were involved in the project, which in later years was used as a workhouse.

1803

The transformation of Arbury Hall with all its Gothic embellishments was complete, including the redesigned gardens, when a more informal picturesque style prevalent in the eighteenth century replaced the formal layout of earlier periods. By this time Arbury's garden was looking quite mature.

1805

The ageing Baronet disclosed his plans for a prize for verse to the Vice-Chancellor of the University of Oxford, Dr Landon. His love of classical architecture and literature inspired this idea of an annual competition for undergraduates with a prize of twenty guineas.

At a cost of £143, Sir Roger ordered a special chandelier for the saloon (the 2002 equivalent value was £5,800) from the London firm Perry and Parker. It was hung as a celebration to mark the end of a remarkable and wonderful lifetime's work here at Arbury Hall. Almost 200 years on, the Baronet's twelve-light lustre illuminates one of his most beautiful and spectacular achievements, the saloon. Cousin Francis Parker was now recognised as the Baronet's heir.

1806

The multi-talented Sir Roger Newdigate, fifth Baronet, died a lonely old gentleman on 25 November, aged eighty-seven. He had achieved so much in his lifetime, and his name stands today as one of the Newdigate family's most distinguished and innovative characters.

During a fifty-year period he created, out of a simple red-brick Elizabethan manor house, the most beautiful early Gothic revival house in all England.

Although married twice, Sir Roger died without issue, and so after 129 years the Baronetcy became extinct.

The estate devolved to Francis Parker, who assumed the Newdigate name and became Francis Parker Newdigate. When he arrived at Arbury, the new owner brought along his own land agent from Kirk Hallam in Derbyshire, the young Robert Evans.

Sir Roger Newdigate, fifth Baronet, by George Romney

Charles Parker and his wife, Jane Anstruther.
Charles was Sir Roger Newdigate's protégé while Jane demolished Harefield Manor in 1813.

1809

Harriet Evans, first wife of agent Robert Evans, died and was buried at Astley.

1813

(A19) Four years on and Astley Church was the venue for Mr Evans' second marriage, this time on 8 February to local girl Christiana Pearson. The couple were to live at a farm on Arbury, today known as South Farm.

(B3) The very same year in Middlesex saw the demise of Harefield Place, which was completely demolished by its owner Jane, widow of Charles Parker. Only the coach house and old walls of the kitchen garden remained as a reminder of its former grandeur.

1816

To Charles Newdigate Parker Newdegate and Maria Boucherett a son was born; he was named Charles and set to become a future heir of Arbury Hall.

1819

On 22 November at 5 a.m. in the morning Christiana Evans gave birth to a daughter at South Farm to be called Mary Ann Evans, who later became known as George Eliot, the Victorian novelist.

1820

There were 310 recorded inhabitants of Astley village.

1825

Mr Francis Parker Newdigate, Master of Arbury, received the gift of a grandson named Edward who was also destined to be a future heir to the estate. His parents were Colonel Francis Newdigate, son of Parker Newdigate, and Lady Barbara Marie Legge, daughter of the third Earl of Dartmouth.

1832

(A19) Colonel Francis Newdigate, who was now resident of Astley Castle, was injured during the election unrest in Nuneaton. The riot act was read from the window of the old Newdegate Arms Inn in the town centre, but despite intervention from the Scots Greys, disturbances went on for two days.

(B3) An unexpected visitor to Dewes Farm, Harefield was King William IV, whom it is said spent a night there after losing his way returning to Windsor.

(C15) An incident at Arbury led to two men being executed at Warwick. On 15 January a gang of twenty poachers were busy taking game belonging to Francis Parker Newdigate from Park Wood on the estate, when confronted by Simon Clay, the gamekeeper. Poachers spotted Mr Clay approaching when he was fired at by nineteen-year-old Robert Twigger. The gamekeeper fell to the ground, where he was struck in the face with the butt of a gun, leaving him senseless.

At the hearing on 31 March, Henry Parker, Robert Twigger and four other men were charged with intent to murder or grievous bodily harm.

Found guilty, Robert Twigger and Henry Parker were executed at Warwick on Saturday, 21 April for poaching and firing on Simon Clay.

The gamekeeper eventually recovered after spending ten days on the danger list.

1835

The twenty-nine-year reign of Francis Parker Newdigate came to an end when he died in Leamington. His great-nephew Charles Newdigate-Newdegate, who was in his twentieth year, succeeded him at Arbury. Charles was also a grandson of the late Sir Roger Newdigate's one-time protégé, Charles Parker.

Little had changed during Francis Parker Newdigate's time at Arbury – probably it didn't need to, for Mr Newdigate had enjoyed the privilege of living in the sumptuous surroundings of the late Baronet's newly completed Gothic mansion. Not everyone, it appears, was sorry to see him go, for a local diarist writing at the time of his death discredited his character with the following quote:

> ...said to have died worth ½ million of money. He was a despicable character, bad feeling landlord, a violator of his word and promises, particularly with his tenantry who he ejected from his farms without mercy.
>
> Universally hated as a tyrant ought to be, and detested by the honest that knew him of all parties.

He may have had a streak of John Newdegate of the late sixteenth century in him.

The Victorian Age

1837

During the same year that Queen Victoria succeeded to the throne, Charles Newdigate-Newdegate came of age and duly inherited the Arbury Estates. Charles was the son of the late Charles Newdigate Parker Newdegate and his wife Maria Bouchette of Willington and Stallingborough in Lincolnshire.

1841

Charles rather generously paid for a complete restoration of St Mary's Church, Harefield, at a personal cost of more than £3,000. The south aisle was extended westwards by two bays, and a tiny eighteenth century portico was replaced by the present porch; all work was of a high quality and faithful to the original.

1843

At the by-election on 10 March, Charles Newdigate-Newdegate embarked on a very long and successful political life when he won the North Warwickshire seat for the Conservative party. The new master of Arbury was also a very keen agriculturalist, and these two interests were to dominate his time in Warwickshire.

1845

At Astley Church, incumbent for five years John Price was replaced with Robert Freeman.

1848

A team of six explorers led by John Septimus Roe discovered an area of land south-east of Perth in Western Australia, which is

South Farm, Arbury, George Eliot's birthplace in 1819

today known as Newdegate in the Shire of Lake Grace. At the time Roe reported that the area was unfit for any useful purpose.

1850

Chilvers Coton railway station opened on 2 September.

1851

Amazingly, the severed head of the Duke of Suffolk, Sir Henry Grey, was discovered almost 300 years after his execution for treason back in 1554.

No one seems to know why the head was not buried along with his body at the time. It was discovered in a vault close to the altar at the Church of the Holy Trinity in the Minories, very close to the site of the Duke's former town house.

The head had been located in almost perfect condition, apparently preserved by the effects of tannin in the sawdust within the vault.

1854

(A9) Although the Crimean War had begun in 1853, British involvement did not begin until Allied forces landed at Alma on 14 September 1854, and the siege of Servastapol, Balaklava and Inkerman began.

(B15) Lt General Sir Edward Newdigate-Newdegate, cousin of Arbury squire Charles, saw active service in the Crimean War, with the Second Battalion of the Rifle Brigade.

(C8) Former Astley incumbent Robert Freeman went to the Crimea to serve as Chaplain to the Light Cavalry Brigade during their campaign.

(D15) One of the most notable achievements of Charles Newdigate-Newdegate's political career was marked at this time when he received a gift of a silver statue engraved as follows:

> Presented to Charles Newdigate-Newdegate Esq., MP, by the members of the Military Arms Trade, in grateful acknowledgement of his exertions, especially during the session of Parliament 1853–54.
> Whereby they were enabled to prove their ability to furnish

The south façade, Arbury Hall

an adequate supply of arms for the public service without assistance from foreign sources, or from a government factory.

This very impressive silver trophy depicts a scene from the famous 'Battle of Inkerman' and still graces Arbury Hall to this day.

1855

Incumbent Robert Freeman dies in the Crimea.

1857

Local novelist George Eliot, who spent the first twenty years of her life living on the edge of Arbury Estate, produced her first fictional novel, *Scenes of Clerical Life*. Sir Roger Newdigate's Gothic extravaganza obviously inspired some of her early work, and in the second of a trilogy of stories, 'Mr Gilfil's Love Story', the Baronet is portrayed as Sir Christopher Cheveral, and his wonderful home as Cheveral Manor. Astley Church also featured under the name of Knebley Church, and its castle as Knebley Abbey.

1862

New Year's Eve saw the birth of future master of Arbury, Sir Francis Newdigate-Newdegate, to Lt Colonel Francis Newdigate and his first wife Charlotte Woodford, daughter of Field Marshall Sir Alexander Woodford GCB GCMG. This event was preceded six months earlier by the birth of Sir Francis' future wife Elizabeth Sophia Lucia, daughter of the third Baron Bagot of Blithefield Hall in Staffordshire.

1866

With the death of Charlotte Woodford, Sir Francis lost his mother at the age of four.

1870

At the age of eighty-eight came the death of Field Marshall Sir Alexander Woodford on 26 August. The father-in-law of Sir Francis had a most distinguished military career going back to

Waterloo, and is remembered in the Royal Garrison Church in Portsmouth with a pew plaque.

1872

It is recorded that at this time Charles Newdigate-Newdegate owned 5,318 acres of land in the Midlands, and almost 1,500 acres in Middlesex.

1874

Captain Barnett was residing at Astley Castle.

1875

Thanks to the generosity of the Rt Hon. Charles Newdigate-Newdegate, restoration work began on St Mary's Church, Astley. It included a beautiful oak-panelled ceiling, ornamented with rich bosses, displaying a variety of coats of arms. There are those of the families associated with the church, including the founder Sir Thomas Astley. In all there are twenty-one shields with six of them devoted to the Newdegate family.

1878

(A8) The work on St Mary's took around three years to complete and was carried out to great satisfaction by Mr Penrose, consulting architect to St Paul's Cathedral.

Astley Church finally reopened for worship on 17 October when Edward Ford was the incumbent.

(B30)During the same year Oscar Wilde won the Newdigate Prize for Verse at Oxford University, with an entry entitled 'Ravenna'. The competition, which is a memorial to the fifth Baronet, was awarded by the university's Professor of Poetry. The award carried a prize of twenty guineas, but some years was not presented if the professor was not sufficiently impressed.

1879

Sir Edward saw service in South Africa during the Zulu Wars.

Charles Newdigate-Newdegate by T Say

1880

(A3) W S Gilbert was a tenant of Breakspeare House, Harefield, and it is said that he wrote his famous 'Yeoman of the Guard' there.

(B19) Local novelist George Eliot died on 22 December, aged sixty-one. The author, who was born at Arbury Farm, was buried at Highgate Cemetery.

(C22) Arbury estate at this time covered approximately half the land area of the parish of Chilvers Coton.

1882

The Rt Hon. Charles Newdigate-Newdegate agreed a thirty-five-year lease of land and mineral rights of part of the Arbury estates to the Griff Mining company.

One of Charles' avid pastimes was riding to hounds, and on one occasion he fell from his horse as it seized with a fit. It is a fact that he very quickly recovered, remounted and continued the chase, such was his enthusiasm.

1885

The Rt Hon. Charles Newdigate-Newdegate stepped down from public life. He retired from politics relinquishing his position as MP for North Warwickshire after an amazingly successful run of forty-two years.

1886

On 9 January, a fire was recorded at Astley Castle.

Sir Francis Newdigate-Newdegate secured victory for Nuneaton Conservatives at the local elections.

1887

The death of the Rt Hon. Charles Newdigate-Newdegate occurred on 16 April. During his very long and successful life as a politician, he made many friends and was held in the highest esteem with politicians of all parties. A keen agriculturalist, he was also very generous to the church, funding restoration work at Harefield and Astley, and with gifts to the church in the village of Hawton in Nottinghamshire.

Charles was sadly missed by people at all levels of society, and following the tarnished image of his predecessor he more than made good the family name. Mr Newdegate did not marry and with his death the estates passed to his cousin Lt General Sir Edward Newdigate-Newdegate.

1888

The year after inheriting Arbury Hall, Sir Edward was made Governor and Commander-in-Chief of Bermuda, succeeding Thomas Lionel John Galway.

A Mr C L Adderly was residing at Astley Castle, while during the same year Griff Colliery number four opened.

1891

The Astley old oak tree, where legend has it Sir Henry Grey was in hiding in 1554, finally blew down in a gale. The Duke of Suffolk's oak and deer hide marquetry table and chair, which is still on view in the Gallery at Arbury Hall, was apparently used in the hollow of the tree. A stone mound now marks the spot at Astley where the historic tree stood.

1892

After a spell of four years Sir Edward Newdigate-Newdegate relinquished his position as Governor of Bermuda and returned to Arbury. He was succeeded by Thomas Casey Lyons.

At the local elections Sir Edward's nephew, Sir Francis Newdigate-Newdegate, was successfully returned as Conservative MP for Nuneaton.

1893

Bermuda, a new local mining village, was built to accommodate miners and their families working at Griff Clara. It was probably named Bermuda after Lt General Sir Edward Newdigate-Newdegate's governorship of Bermuda at that time. The village had seventy new cottages built at an approximate cost of £100

A stone cairn now marks the spot where the Duke of Suffolk was captured in 1554

The Duke of Suffolk's oak and deer-hide chair and table, used in his escape bid in 1554

each. A direct route into Arbury Park from the settlement is known as Harefield Lane.

On 9 March, Lt Colonel Francis Newdigate – father of the new Nuneaton MP – died at the age of seventy-one. The Colonel's widow, his second wife, was the Hon. Louisa Georgina Leigh; his first wife was Charlotte Woodford. He was buried at Astley. Towards the end of his life the Colonel had lived at Allesley Park in Coventry. During the same year Francis A N Newdegate had annexed a new wing to his residence, Weston in Arden Hall at Bulkington.

1896

The Rt Hon. Lucia Charlotte Susan Newdegate was born on 6 October, daughter of MP Francis Alexander Newdigate-Newdegate and his wife the Hon. Elizabeth Bagot, daughter of the third Baron Bagot of Blithefield Hall, Staffordshire.

1897

Sir Francis Alexander Newdigate-Newdegate was appointed Deputy Lieutenant of Warwickshire.

Commander John Maurice FitzRoy was born on 20 March, just five months after his future bride, the Hon. Lucia C S Newdegate. John, son of Captain Edward Algernon FitzRoy and Murial Douglas-Pennant was born in Chelsea, London.

1898

(A3) Harefield finally received its title and parish status.

(B22) In Nuneaton on 18 June, Sir Francis Alexander Newdigate-Newdegate MP laid the foundation stone for the new Nuneaton Conservative Club in Bondgate.

1899

The Church of the Holy Trinity in the Minories was demolished, and the head of the executed Sir Henry Grey was removed to St Botolphs, Aldgate. It was stored for a while in a cupboard before its eventual reburial. The head had been used as a rather gory display for fascinated Victorians.

1901

(A15) Just prior to inheriting Arbury Hall, Francis Alexander Newdigate-Newdegate took brief residence at Astley Castle.

(B9) At Osborne House on the Isle of Wight, the Victorian era came to an end when the Queen died aged eighty-one on 22 January.

Queen Victoria was succeeded by her son, Edward VII.

Lt General Sir Edward Newdigate-Newdegate by W Miller

The Edwardian Age

1902

On 1 August, Lt General Sir Edward Newdigate-Newdegate passed away aged seventy-seven.

Sir Edward's widow was Anne Emily Garnier, daughter of the very Rev. Thomas Garnier, Dean of Lincoln. The General had been Master of Arbury for fifteen years, and was buried in the church cemetery of St Mary the Virgin, Astley.

In the church, the General is remembered by a modern stained-glass memorial window in the south wall; his military distinction is also reflected in the Rifle Brigades roll of fame at Winchester Cathedral.

The Arbury estates devolved on his nephew, Nuneaton MP Francis Alexander Newdigate-Newdegate, who at the time was thirty-nine years of age.

1903

The new owner of Arbury Hall, Francis, presented two beautiful Venetian lamp standards, each standing over six feet high, to St Mary's Church, Astley.

Today they can be seen placed either side of the altar.

1905

(A8) Francis was also responsible for relocating three alabaster figures in the church into their present positions. The recumbent effigies, of Sir Edward Grey, Elizabeth Talbot, Viscountess Lisle and Cecily the Marchioness of Dorset, were damaged survivors from the church disaster of 1600.

(B15) He also made another gift, this time a Flemish triptych depicting the taking down of our blessed Lord from the cross.

Francis Alexander Newdigate-Newdegate MP entertained

Harefield village, 1905. Picture courtesy of Jean Lapworth.

A fair on Harefield Green, 1905. Picture courtesy of Jean Lapworth.

General Redvers Buller VC at Arbury on the occasion of the unveiling of a Boer War memorial at Bondgate Nuneaton on 28 January. The event was preceded by a procession through town of military and local dignitaries.

The red carpet on the floor of the cloister at Arbury Hall is said to have been laid for the General's visit. (The famous red carpet was replaced, after an amazing one-hundred-and-one-year period, in April 2006, with a beige one.)

1906

Following a sequence of fourteen years as MP for Nuneaton, Francis Alexander Newdigate-Newdegate lost his seat to rival William Johnson, the successful Lib/Lab candidate receiving massive support as agent to the Warwickshire Miners' Association.

1909

Francis Alexander Newdigate-Newdegate rekindled his political career when he successfully stood as Conservative candidate for Tamworth.

1910

Francis doubled the size of the windows in Astley Church.

1914

During the summer, the first world war began. Britain declared war on 4 August against Austria and Hungary.

In November, Mr and Mrs Charles Billyard-Leake, Australians resident in England, offered Harefield Park, Middlesex as a home for convalescent and wounded soldiers of the AIF. It was duly accepted by the Commonwealth Defence Department on 14 December.

1915

The official opening of the Australian Auxiliary Hospital at Harefield Park took place on 4 June.

The hospital's first Commanding Officer was Captain M V Southey AAMC. The function of the depot was essentially to be a rest home to recuperate after sickness or injury for military personnel, and a depot for collecting invalids for return to Australia.

King George V and Queen Mary visited the hospital on 16 August.

The Hon. Lucia Charlotte Susan Newdegate, now a nineteen-year-old debutante, sat for the Belgian artist Jonniaux for a full-length portrait in her deb's dress – a painting which adorns the saloon at Arbury to this day.

The House of Windsor

1917

(A15) Francis Alexander Newdigate-Newdegate ended a run of eight years as MP for Tamworth when he was appointed Governor of Tasmania.

At Harefield, military funerals were conducted for those who died at the hospital, with burials taking place at St Mary's churchyard.

(B3) A new Australian cemetery was made on ground given to the church by Francis Alexander Newdigate-Newdegate, reserved for Australian soldiers. Mr Newdegate also paid expenses for the burials excluding the coffins, which were provided by the AIF.

(C15) Life at Arbury was very much affected by the war, as the Hall also became a hospital for treating wounded soldiers.

1918

By the time the First World War had ended, a total of 111 Australian soldiers had been buried at Harefield, along with one nursing sister who died during the campaign.

1919

(A3) The hospital gradually closed during the year as the effects of war subsided. An extensive list of important visitors, including HRH the Duke of Connaught, the Dowager Marchioness of Linlithgow, the Bishop of Kensington, the Rt Hon. Andrew Fisher (High Commissioner), Francis Alexander Newdigate-Newdegate (Governor elect of Tasmania) and Lady Newdegate, had visited the hospital during its lifetime.

(B15) On 21 May, the marriage took place of Francis Newdegate's daughter Lucia Charlotte Susan Newdegate to John Maurice FitzRoy, third son of the Hon. Edward Algernon FitzRoy and his wife Murial Douglas-Pennant. The FitzRoys are descendants of Henry FitzRoy, first Duke of Grafton.

1920

(A15) Francis Alexander Newdigate-Newdegate relinquished his position as Governor of Tasmania to become Governor of Western Australia.

He also became a grandfather on 28 March when his daughter Lucia gave birth to a girl, who was named Lucia Anne FitzRoy.

(B3) Incumbent at Harefield Church was H S Cochan.

1921

(A15) On 17 December, a son and heir to Arbury was born to the Rt Hon. Lucia and John FitzRoy. He was named Francis Humphrey Maurice FitzRoy.

(B3) At Harefield Australian Cemetery, Mr Billyard Leake and Lord of the Manor Francis Alexander Newdigate-Newdegate erected a granite obelisk as a memorial to Australian soldiers.

1924

Francis Alexander Newdigate-Newdegate retired as governor of Western Australia.

The year also saw the death of Anne Emily Garnier, widow of the late Lt General Sir Edward Newdigate-Newdegate.

1925

Sir Francis Alexander Newdigate-Newdegate was knighted, a just reward for a most distinguished career.

His son-in-law, John Maurice FitzRoy made his debut for Northamptonshire at cricket. Johns county career lasted three seasons and his personal first class record was as follows:

Batting

Matches:	56
Innings:	101
Not Out:	6
Runs:	1,373

Highest Score: 50
Average: 14.45

Bowling
    Balls: 143
    Maidens: 4
    Runs: 82
    Wickets: 6
    Average: 13.66

John was a right-hand bat and he also held forty-seven catches.

1926

(A3) Sir Francis Alexander Newdigate-Newdegate sold off another piece of old Harefield when he disposed of the land on which stood the 800-year-old Chapel of Moorhall. It was once a thriving part of a Preceptor of the Knights Hospitallers of St John of Jerusalem.

(B27) A region south-east of Perth in Western Australia, first discovered by the intrepid explorer John Septimus Roe, was finally cleared and named Newdegate after the former Governor Sir Francis Alexander Newdigate-Newdegate. The area, originally feared to be of little use, is today a thriving farming region which annually stages the Newdegate Field Day in September. This is an event which hosts one of the best displays of field machinery in Western Australia.

(C15) The future bride of Francis Humphrey Maurice FitzRoy Newdegate was born on 28 March, the Hon. Rosemary Norrie, daughter of Charles Willoughby Moke Norrie and Jocelyn Helen Gosling.

1927

(A8) 19 August was indeed a momentous occasion in the history of Arbury Hall and Astley, with the visit of Her Majesty Queen Mary, as part of her stay in the Midlands. Rev. Ivo Carr-Gregg MA, FRAS, Vicar of Astley and author of that wonderful book *The History of Astley and its Parish Church*, described the visit thus:

What a special privilege to have had the great honour of receiving the Queen of England in the parish church. It was [apparently a quote from the Parish Magazine] a memorable red-letter day in the annals of the parish. The sunny and beautiful afternoon will remain as a happy memory with all those who were present that day when the Royal lady came among us, and won all our hearts by her gracious and kindly personality. I shall long treasure the words of thanks she spoke to me at the conclusion of her visit.

(B15) Two maturing oak trees growing in the gardens of Arbury Hall were planted by royal guests to commemorate their visits. The first was planted on 19 August 1927 by HRH Queen Mary, and the second by the Prince of Wales (later Edward VIII) on 10 July 1934. Both were guests of Sir Francis Alexander Newdigate-Newdegate.

1928

When the English poet and writer Siegfried Sassoon published his country classic, *Memoirs of a Fox Hunting Man*, it was the second time in Newdegate history that the family had appeared under a pseudonym. Sir Roger Newdigate had appeared in George Eliot's novel *Scenes of Clerical Life* as Sir Christopher Cheveral. This time Sir Francis Alexander Newdigate-Newdegate was depicted as Sir Jocelyn Porteus-Porteous of Frolesford Hall (Arbury Hall), King of the Saturday Country for the Packlestone (Atherstone) hunt. In the book Sir Jocelyn is described as of pompous nature, with a lofty and impercipient attitude towards the plebeian upstarts who lived outside his grandiose gateway.

The Saturday Country was described as the least popular of the four divisions, well-wooded, hilly and blemished by collieries.

The father-in-law of Sir Francis Alexander Newdigate-Newdegate's daughter Lucia, Rt Hon. Edward Algernon FitzRoy, was made Speaker of the House. The FitzRoys were descendants of the first Duke of Grafton, Henry FitzRoy (1817–1877).

1929

Jocelyne FitzRoy Newdegate was born on 13 July, third child of

Lucia Charlotte Susan Newdigate-Newdegate, 1915, by R Jonniaux

The third Viscount Daventry by Marcus May

the Hon. John Maurice FitzRoy and his wife the Hon. Lucia
Charlotte Susan FitzRoy-Newdegate.

1930

At the age of eight, Humphrey FitzRoy-Newdegate was sent to
school in Reigate, Surrey. During this period Astley Church
football team played locally in the original Bible Class League.

For a number of years cricket was also played in the village
before a shortage of players led to the team being disbanded.

1934

The grand new Nuneaton Council House was officially opened
by Sir Francis Alexander Newdigate-Newdegate on 26 April.

1935

At the age of thirteen Humphrey FitzRoy continued his education
at Eton.

1936

(A15) The year began sadly with the death on 2 January of Sir Francis
Alexander Newdigate-Newdegate at the age of seventy-three.

(B36) Arbury and the family estates passed to his daughter, the
Rt Hon. Mrs Lucia Charlotte Susan FitzRoy-Newdegate, wife of
Commander John Maurice FitzRoy.

With this event the family name of FitzRoy-Newdegate took
its present form.

The accession of King Edward VIII took place on 10 January,
with the death of George V. However King Edward reigned only 325
days before the Rt Hon. Edward Algernon FitzRoy, as Speaker of the
House, announced his abdication to Parliament on 10 December.

With the death of Sir Francis Alexander Newdigate-
Newdegate, large areas of land had to be sold off, to relieve the
family's burden of death duties. This also included the remainder
of the Newdegate's Harefield Estates, which were sold to
Middlesex County Council. A general recession in farming must
have made this a most difficult period.

1939

It was announced by the Speaker of the House, the Rt Hon. Edward Algernon FitzRoy, at 11 a.m. on 3 September, that as from 5 p.m. Britain was at war with Germany.

1940

Humphrey FitzRoy-Newdegate left Eton school and joined the Young Soldiers Battalion, who were mostly East-Enders from London. One of their duties was to guard Willesden Station.

In the autumn German planes dropped bombs during air raids on Arbury woods, Griff Hollows, Griff House cottage and the Heath End Road area on 29 October, and later on 14 November near North Lodge at the Round Towers, and on 19 November at Bermuda.

On 29 December came the death of Sir Francis Alexander Newdigate-Newdegate's widow, the seventy-eight-year-old Elizabeth Sophia Lucia, daughter of the third Baron Bagot of Blithefield in Staffordshire.

1941

During May, extensive damage was caused locally by more German bombing raids, and Coton Church was a major casualty on 17 May.

Bombs also landed near Griff Lodge and Coton Lawn Farm on 5 and 12 June respectively.

1942

A German Dornier bomber crash-landed near Bermuda village, and its crew of four were taken prisoner.

1943

(A34) Speaker of the House the Rt Hon. Edward Algernon FitzRoy died on 2 March at the age of seventy-three. FitzRoy's funeral was held in St Margaret's Church, Westminster, where he was buried in the Chancel. King George VI bestowed the title

Viscountess Daventry on his widow Muriel Douglas-Pennant in her own right, in recognition of her late husband's very successful period of office between 1928 and 1943.

(B28) The death of Sir Francis Alexander Newdigate-Newdegate had brought crippling death duties to Arbury, which resulted in a massive sale of land, mainly south of Arbury Park.

On Tuesday, 12 January at the Bull Hotel Nuneaton, ten agricultural holdings and two coppices were auctioned by Nixon, Toone and Harrison on the instruction of the personal representatives of the late Sir Francis and of Mrs FitzRoy Newdegate. In all there were thirteen lots, a total of 1,066 acres of land. Before the sale the size of Arbury Estates had been considerably more than 6,000 acres.

Now at the height of the second world war, Mrs FitzRoy Newdegate continued to live in a small corner of Arbury Hall, even though the place had been virtually taken over by the army. First British regiments, then American, before finally the estate was used as a Prisoner of War camp for German soldiers.

Her son Mr Humphrey FitzRoy Newdegate (later to become third Viscount Daventry) was now serving in the Coldstream Guards, taking part in their campaigns in North Africa and Tunisia. He was also twice wounded landing in Italy.

The army had also taken over Astley Castle, using it as a reception camp and recuperation centre for soldiers before they returned to their units.

1945

As the second world war came to an end, Arbury was home to a staggering 10,000 German prisoners, with wooden huts littering every part of the park.

Both Arbury Hall gardens and park and Astley Castle suffered serious damage during the occupation, and an enormous task awaited the family. Even Temple House had been used by the army. Mercifully, although many German bombs had fallen in the area, Sir Roger Newdigate's Gothic gem had miraculously survived.

Humphrey M FitzRoy Newdegate travelled to India as aide-de-camp to the Viceroy Field Marshall Lord Wavell.

Lord Wavell was Viceroy of India from 1943 until its independence in 1947.

1946

(A28) On inspection Astley Castle was found to be around four feet under water after taps had been left running. This damage only added to the misery of the aftermath.

(B31) Over at Arbury, among the many German prisoners were enough skilled tradesmen to make a significant impact on rebuilding the bomb-damaged All Saints Church, Chilvers Coton. Work commenced under the inspirational leadership of the Rev. R T Murray.

1947

(A31) Following the restoration work All Saints Church was re-consecrated in September.

(B28) Sadly the castle now stood empty, even its contents had been removed to Arbury. This historic building that had been acquired by the family way back in the seventeenth century had been used much of the time principally as a second home for members of the family. The last to live there had been Lady Newdegate, widow of Sir Francis Alexander Newdigate-Newdegate, who had spent around a year living there prior to her death in 1940.

1950

Mr Francis Humphrey Maurice FitzRoy Newdegate returned home from overseas to find Arbury in a terrible state following the war. Being a Prisoner of War camp had clearly taken its toll, with damage and dilapidation everywhere. Even though Arbury Hall narrowly escaped Hitler's bombs, this must have been one of the most vulnerable periods in its history.

The late Lord Daventry stated that 'the place was an absolute wreck.'

The family faced a long and tedious struggle to save the Hall and restore the Estate to something like its former glory. At this stage the owner, the Hon. Mrs Lucia C S FitzRoy Newdegate signed the estates over to her son Humphrey.

1951

(A3) At Harefield, the Breakspeare Chapel in St Mary's Church was dedicated as a memorial chapel to Australian soldiers who lost their lives during the war.

The Rev. K T Toole-Mackson was the incumbent.

(B28) Arbury's new owner was already involved in an early conservation battle to prevent the National Coal Board extracting coal from fifty acres of land beneath the hall. The NCB's plans also put the future of Astley Church in jeopardy with similar ambitions. However, Arbury won on both counts when Harold Macmillan, Minister for Housing and Local Government, surprisingly intervened in Arbury's favour. It proved a landmark in the history of the conservation movement, but how ironical considering the grand house had been built on the profits of a coal mine.

As part of the Festival of Britain celebrations, a Pageant of Astley was staged in the gardens of Astley Castle. Written by its vicar, the multi-talented Rev. Ivo Carr-Gregg, the pageant re-enacted Astley's rich history from Saxon times through the turbulent medieval period to the dissolution of its collegiate establishment in 1545. Major parts were played by members of the Nuneaton Dramatic Society.

The Povey Harpers were resident in the castle.

1952

(A2) As a precaution for its safety and future, the Rev. Ivo Carr-Gregg won the right to have Astley Church underpinned with a new raft foundation of concrete and steel to allow for the extraction of coal from beneath the building. The church held a special re-opening service on 25 September when the Bishop of Coventry, Dr Neville Gorton, praised the vicar's courageous battle.

(B9) With the death of King George VI in February, Britain entered a new era.

Reflections of Arbury Hall

The Second Elizabethan Period

1953

(A15) The coronation year of Queen Elizabeth II marked the beginning of a new era for Arbury Hall. The Depression, followed by the second world war, had taken its toll on grand country houses all over England. In the decade after the war some 400 of them were demolished and a whole lot more were in severe financial trouble.

The new owner of Arbury, Francis Humphrey Maurice FitzRoy Newdegate (later to become third Viscount Daventry), made a vital decision to safeguard Arbury's future when he accepted a grant to repair damaged stonework from the Historic Buildings Association on the condition that the beautiful historically important Hall be opened to the public. In the early days hundreds of people would visit Arbury on a Sunday afternoon to see Sir Roger Newdigate's Gothic dream, often welcomed in person by the owner's mother, the Hon. Mrs Lucia C S FitzRoy Newdegate.

(B28) In fact the Hon. Mrs L C S FitzRoy Newdegate had quite a year, for she was honoured to be Mayoress of Nuneaton Borough. A glass with a silver three-penny piece moulded into it is on display in the Hall to commemorate the occasion, a gift from the Borough Council.

The future father-in-law of Mr Humphrey FitzRoy Newdegate, Lt General Sir Charles Willoughby Moke Norrie GCMG, GCNO, CB, DSO, MC, KSTJ was Governor of New Zealand 1952–1957. He entertained Her Majesty Queen Elizabeth II and Prince Phillip when they visited New Zealand during their coronation-year tour of the Commonwealth.

1955

After a productive life of sixty-four years, the local colliery known as Griff Clara closed down.

1956

The Vicar of Astley, Rev. Ivo Carr-Gregg, died in early June in his eightieth year. His funeral at St Mary the Virgin was conducted by Canon J B Sinker of Nuneaton on the morning of 8 June.

The late Bishop of Coventry paid tribute to a great man who had been incumbent at Astley for thirty-nine years.

Rev. Ivo Carr-Gregg was born in Reigate, Surrey, and during his time at Astley wrote that wonderful book *The History of Astley and its Church*. He also escorted Queen Mary around the church when she paid Astley a visit in 1927.

1958

Astley Castle, which had been a Newdegate family home for almost 300 years, was now leased as an hotel. The first proprietors were Mr and Mrs Tunnicliffe, who opened a very comfortable establishment. One of the first functions was a Whit Monday dance in aid of High View Hospital Exhall. Tickets were 2/6d.

1959

On 20 October, the marriage took place between Francis Humphrey Maurice FitzRoy Newdegate, son of John Maurice and the Hon. Mrs Lucia C S FitzRoy Newdegate, and the Hon. Rosemary Norrie, daughter of the first Baron Norrie, Sir Charles Willoughby, and Jocelyn Helen Gosling. The couple made their home at Temple House in Arbury Park.

However, due to Temple House having major problems with death-watch beetle, the newlyweds were forced to rent a property in the beautiful Oxfordshire Village of Churchill while the problem was being rectified.

1960

(A2) After emerging from a four-year sequestration period, St Mary the Virgin Church at Astley was united with All Saints Church, Chilvers Coton to become one ecclesiastical parish. Rev. Pierpoint-Rigby was the incumbent.

(B28) A new heir to the Arbury Estates was born on 27 July:

The home pool at Arbury Hall

James Edward FitzRoy Newdegate, eldest son of Humphrey M FitzRoy Newdegate and his wife, the Hon. Rosemary Norrie.

James was christened at All Saints Church in Churchill.

(C30) The poet John Fuller was the recipient of the Newdegate prize for verse at Oxford University with 'A Dialogue between Caliban and Ariel'.

(D3) At Harefield, Uxbridge Council demolished one of the oldest buildings in the parish, the ancient Manor of Moorhall.

Almost 800 years ago the Hall was part of a thriving Preceptor of the Knights Hospitallers of St John of Jerusalem.

At the Dissolution, Henry VIII granted Moorhall to Robert Tyrwhit, who conveyed it to John Newdegate. It has passed with the Manor of Harefield ever since.

Much restored, it survived as an ancient monument, for years being used as a chapel, mission room, granary and finally a cattle shed.

(E28) Captain Humphrey FitzRoy Newdegate, Justice of the Peace, became a magistrate, in the early days at Nuneaton sitting for one morning every two weeks.

1961

(A2) An archaeological dig at St Mary the Virgin Church, Astley, revealed during the excavations part of the footings of the North Transept, which was part of the original much larger Collegiate Church dating from 1343.

(B28) With Astley Castle now in use as a hotel, the more affluent sixties enabled it to flourish under the Tunnicliffe and eventually the Challinor families. It became a very popular venue for local families to celebrate special occasions, with wedding receptions a speciality.

1962

On 8 July, the death occurred of Viscountess Daventry, Muriel Douglas-Pennant, widow of the late Speaker, FitzRoy. The Viscountess was in her ninety-third year and the title passed to her son Oliver FitzRoy.

The title must now pass through the male line of the family.

Hugh Francis FitzRoy Newdegate was born on 4 October, a second son for Mr Humphrey Maurice and the Hon. Rosemary FitzRoy Newdegate, and a brother for James. Hugh was baptised at St Mary the Virgin, Astley by Rev. Pierpoint Rigby on Sunday, 16 December.

1964

A third and final child to the Newdegates of Arbury arrived when daughter Joanne Norrie was born on 8 February.

1965

(A28) Georgia, a future Viscountess and Lady Newdegate, was born, daughter of Mr John Lodge of Daglingworth Place in Gloucestershire.

(B30) 'Fear' by Peter Jay, was the winner of the Newdigate Prize at Oxford University. Each year the Professor of Poetry at Oxford chooses a title, traditionally the material narrative paintings are made of descriptive poetry of the classical type, then judges the best entry. The author then reads it as part of the annual Encaenia ceremony.

1968

The modern poet James Fenton proved to be the next winner of the Newdigate Prize with his entry 'The Opening of Japan'.

1969

The 150th anniversary celebration of the birth on Arbury of our local world-famous novelist George Eliot took place in Astley Church between 20 and 23 June.

Entitled 'Scenes from the works of George Eliot, immortalised in flowers', the popular event was a wonderful way to commemorate the occasion.

1970

During April, Mr Humphrey FitzRoy Newdegate was honoured to be made High Sheriff of Warwickshire.

On Sunday 9 August, Arbury Estates staged probably the biggest outdoor event in its history when hosting the British Field Sports Society's Annual Country Fair.

Many thousands of visitors from all walks of life descended on the beautiful Arbury Park to join in a truly memorable occasion. All field sports from the world of hunting, shooting and fishing plus many minority sports were well represented. The summer weather was at its best, and a wonderful day was enjoyed by all.

1971

At the Bull Ring, Chilvers Coton, the former college for the poor originally built by Sir Roger Newdigate in 1800 was demolished to make space for the George Eliot Hospital expansions.

Following the Poor Law Act in 1834 the grim stone building became a workhouse and was latterly known as Coton Lodge Home for the Old Folks.

1973

(A29) 21 July became a sad day in the history of Astley with the closure of the village school. Since 1948 it had been both an infants and junior school, but eventually suffered the same fate as many other English village schools.

(B30) At Oxford, entrant Nicholas Poussin stated that the Newdigate Prize was so badly advertised (i.e. not at all) that most undergraduates weren't aware it even existed. The instructions, if you could find them, were pleasantly odd.

However, enough undergraduates did find them to allow the Professor of Poetry to consistently award the prize through the middle years of the 1970s to the following contestants:

1972:   'The Ancestral Face' by Neil Rhodes
1973:   'The Wife's Tale' by Christopher Mann
1974:   'Death of a Poet' by Alan Hollinghurst
1975:   'The Tides' by Andrew Motion
1976:   'Hostages' by David Winzar
1977:   'The Fool' by Michael King

In 1978, the hundredth anniversary of Oscar Wilde's winning entry 'Ravenna', the prize was not awarded.

1975–76

The countryside suffered such severe drought conditions during successive long hot summers that, locally, Seaswood Pool shrank to about half its normal size. It evaporated so much it revealed an old brick bridge built near the willow trees, traversing from north to south. Many local people had never previously or since seen the structure. Could it have been there before Sir Roger Newdigate first dammed the lake to its present size in 1764.

1976

On 11 May came the death of the Hon. John Maurice FitzRoy Newdegate at the age of seventy-nine. His widow, the Hon. Mrs Lucia Charlotte Susan FitzRoy Newdegate, continued to live at Arbury Hall.

1977

During the year another sad occasion hit the Newdegate family with the death of Baron Norrie, father of the Hon. Mrs Rosemary FitzRoy Newdegate.

Lt General the Rt Hon. Sir Willoughby Moke Norrie was Governor of Australia between 1944 and 1952, and was created Baron Norrie of Wellington, New Zealand and of Upton, Gloucestershire when he then came to New Zealand.

Following his retirement he became Chancellor of the Most Distinguished Order of St Michael and St George (1960–1968), the British Order associated with overseas and diplomatic services.

1978

During October the Medieval Astley Castle was gutted by fire, on the very day that its lease as a hotel expired. It was the historically important former home to two Queens of England, Elizabeth Woodville, the widow of Sir John Grey, who married Edward IV and was mother to the Princes in the Tower, and daughter Elizabeth of York, plus the tragically unfortunate Lady Jane Grey, who was proclaimed queen for just nine days.

Highpark Pool, Arbury Park

The castle had been used as a second home for the Newdegate family since Richard Newdigate, the first Baronet, bought it in 1674, right through to the second world war.

This terrible disaster shook not only the owners, Arbury Estates, but everyone in the area who held the immensely rich vein of Astley's historic importance close to their hearts.

At Arbury, pheasant shooting stretches back to at least late-Victorian times, and before that a mixed bag of partridge, wood-cock and duck would have been more likely. By 1978, Captain Humphrey Maurice FitzRoy Newdegate simply loved his shooting days. At this particular time he said goodbye to his loyal gamekeeper, Mr Reginald Vernon, who at the age of sixty-five retired to a quieter life after a staggering fifty years being a gamekeeper. This at times funny, if daunting, disciplinarian had been a gamekeeper all his working life, and was replaced on the Estate by a wily Yorkshireman with vast grouse moor experience, Mr Owen Stainthorpe, along with his able wife Sheila.

During Vernon's time the shooting season would begin in September, with a couple of partridge days, and close after the pheasant season ended on 1 February, with a day's hare shooting. On these occasions lunch for the beaters would be enjoyed with a couple of pints in the bar of Astley Castle.

Sadly both the keeper and the hugely popular castle facility disappeared during the same year.

1981

A party was thrown at Arbury Hall to celebrate the twenty-first birthday of the heir to the Estate, the Hon. James Edward FitzRoy Newdegate.

The event on 27 July was attended by family, friends and many of the staff from Arbury.

1982

(A15) Newdigate, the last of the local collieries, finally ceased production following a working life of eighty-four years. During its time the down shaft was nicknamed 'Frankie's', after Sir Francis Alexander Newdigate-Newdegate, while the up shaft was known as 'Lila', after Sir Francis' wife, Elizabeth.

The death of the Hon. Mrs Lucia Charlotte Susan FitzRoy Newdegate JP on 10 September was indeed another dark day for the family. The late mother of the Arbury owner Capt. Humphrey FitzRoy Newdegate proved a real stalwart in the early days of her ownership of Arbury, surviving not only the horrific death duties imposed on the Estate at the loss of her own father Sir Francis Newdigate-Newdegate in 1936, but somehow miraculously bringing Arbury through the turbulent years of the second world war.

Mrs FitzRoy Newdegate sat throughout this extremely difficult period of American and British occupation of Arbury, and, even though the scars of the Prisoner of War camp blighted the park for years to come, successfully delivered Arbury to her son in 1950. Ever popular with the local public after holding office as Mayoress of Nuneaton in 1953, the late Mrs FitzRoy Newdegate was in her eighty-sixth year.

A beautiful full-length portrait of her adorns the walls of the Saloon today, painted by the Belgian artist Jonniaux in 1915.

The loss of the Hon. Mrs FitzRoy Newdegate brought to an end, if only temporarily, almost 400 years of Newdegate occupancy of the Hall.

The owner, Captain Humphrey FitzRoy Newdegate, and his family chose to live on at Temple House across the park, leaving administrative staff to live in and manage the historic Hall's future. During this period there appeared to be an upsurge in the many grand events and occasions staged at Arbury, with musical evenings, George Eliot readings and corporate entertaining enjoyed in the Hall.

Out in the park, as well as the traditional country pursuits of hunting, shooting and fishing, many public events such as craft fairs, transport through the years, music and fireworks evenings continued to keep Arbury centre stage. Added to all of this, the Hall and gardens welcomed visitors on almost a daily basis through the summer months.

(B28) At Harefield, the last private estate, known as The Grove, was sold by the Cox family after the death of John and Lavinia.

(C30) Sir Roger's Newdigate Prize at Oxford suffered a lean period during the late 1970s and early '80s. Simon Higginson's 1980 entry 'Inflation in 1980' was the only recipient to receive the prize during a four-year spell. Throughout the '80s then the Prize was awarded to the following:

1982:   'Souvenirs' by Gordon Wattles
1983:   'Triumphs' by Peter McDonald
1984:   'Fear' by James Leader
1985:   'Magic' by Robert Twigger
1986:   'An Epithalamion' by William Morris
1987:   'Memoirs of Tiresias' by Bruce Gibson & Michael Suarez
1988:   'Elegy' by Mark Wormald
1989:   'The House' by Jane Griffiths

1984

Arbury owner Captain Humphrey FitzRoy Newdegate and his wife, the Hon. Rosemary Norrie, celebrated twenty-five years of marriage on 20 October. The Silver Wedding was marked by a gift of a bronze ballerina figure from local sculptor John Letts, which is beautifully displayed in the Hall. John Lett's studio was situated in the old school room at Astley Village, a facility he shared with colleague Keith Lee.

1986

During a year that saw the Newdegate family celebrate 400 years at Arbury, the present owner Humphrey FitzRoy Newdegate became the third Viscount Daventry. The death of his uncle Oliver FitzRoy, the second Viscount Daventry, in his ninety-third year, saw the title pass down through the male line into the Newdegate side of the family.

Viscount is the fourth highest title of honour in the peerage; it used to be customary to honour retiring senior ministers and speakers of the house with a Viscount title, though it is now less frequent.

The first Viscount to be created in 1440 was Viscount Beaumont.

The George Eliot Fellowship, with support from Nuneaton and Bedworth Borough Council, commissioned Astley sculptor John Letts to produce a bronze statue of our much-loved novelist.

As a result a wonderful statue of Nuneaton's favourite daughter in a seated position on a huge plinth was unveiled by Jonathan Ouvry, President of the George Eliot Fellowship, during a civic ceremony on 22 March in Newdegate Square, Nuneaton.

1987

A protest by the people of Chilvers Coton and surrounding areas thwarted plans by the local council to demolish the building previously known as the Free School. The school had operated for the poor children of the area since founded by Lady Newdigate, Elizabeth Twisden, mother of the fifth Baronet, Sir Roger Newdigate, in 1745. In more recent times the school became known as Shepperton Junior School, before changing to its present use as Chilvers Coton Heritage Centre.

At Astley in the late 1980s the rise in the popularity of Hollybush Farm somehow appeared to cushion the effect that the loss of the Castle had on the village. It proved no real compensation, however, but the success of the farming enterprise by the late Ted Hammond did breathe life into the hamlet as people came from nearby towns and villages to pick their own fruit and vegetables and general farm produce. The farm turned back the clock with an old-fashioned stock of animals and birds that proved a wonderful attraction for everyone. Even a deer enclosure in a field by the crossroads added to the interest.

1990

(A28) At the age of sixty-nine, the owner of Arbury Hall, the third Viscount Daventry, Humphrey FitzRoy Newdegate, received the honour of becoming Lord Lieutenant of Warwickshire.

Today it's an office of honour, but still retains a link with reserve forces and also makes recommendations for appointments of justices of the peace.

A Lord Lieutenant is the Sovereign's permanent representative in the county, and originated in 1539 during the reign of Henry VIII.

The beaters at South Farm, Arbury, in the 1980s

The office in those far-off days was responsible for raising a militia in times of civil unrest.

This was indeed a just award, on 2 August, following the Viscount's lifelong dedication to military and public services.

(B30) 'Mapping' by Roderick Clayton was awarded the Newdigate Prize at Oxford University.

Following a blank year in 1991 the award was presented until the mid-nineties to:

1992: 'Green Thought' by Fiona Sampson
1993: 'The Landing' by Caron Rohsler
1994: 'Making Sense' by James Merino
1995: 'Judith with the Head of Holofernes' by Antony Dunn

The Newdigate Prize was not awarded for the rest of the decade.

1994

10 September was a time for great celebration when the heir to Arbury, the Hon. James Edward FitzRoy Newdegate, eldest son of the third Viscount and Viscountess Daventry, married Miss Georgia Lodge, daughter of John Lodge, at Daglingworth Place, Gloucestershire.

The marriage took place at Cirencester Civil Parish Church, St John the Baptist, which is the largest parish church in the county.

The bride came from the beautiful nearby village of Daglingworth, on the fringe of the Earl of Bathhurst's massive country estate.

The summer of '94 in fact turned out very eventful as film-makers Philip and Belinda Haas finally settled on Arbury Hall, gardens and park, as the perfect location for their new film based on a novel by A S Byatt. The couple's frantic search led them to many country houses before they discovered an ideal setting for *Angels and Insects*, and they were completely knocked out by Sir Roger's Gothic gem.

Filming commenced in June and took twelve weeks, completely transforming the normal layout within the Hall. Some of the furniture was used and many items were placed in storage for their safekeeping. Patsy Kensit and Mark Rylance were the stars of this rather creepy Victorian drama, along with Kristin Scott Thomas, Anna Massey, and Jeremy Kemp. Many local people successfully auditioned for minor parts, including staff from Arbury Hall.

Visitors to Arbury were often quite bemused when viewing the Hall that summer, stepping aside cables and lighting equipment, and peering between film sets to snatch a glimpse of Arbury's beautiful interiors.

Everything started to return to tranquil normality when filming was complete around 3 September. The people disappeared; furniture and fine art were returned and some rooms even enjoyed a lick of paint.

A memorable year continued for the Newdegates and Arbury when, on 8 December, Lord Daventry attended Her Majesty Queen Elizabeth II and the Duke of Edinburgh as Lord Lieutenant of Warwickshire on the royal official visit to Nuneaton.

The very proud third Viscount Daventry enjoyed the highlight of his term of office by welcoming the royal party to the town at Trent Valley railway station, before attending them on visits to the George Eliot Hospital and Higham Lane School farm.

The special day concluded when the royal convoy drove past the Viscount's Arbury Estate through Astley village en-route for a further engagement at the Jaguar car plant in Coventry.

1995

(A40) A very special occasion took place on the night of 4 February when HRH Prince Phillip, Duke of Edinburgh, paid a private visit to Temple House, Arbury, as guest of Viscount and Viscountess Daventry en route for Carriage Driving at Stoneleigh Abbey.

A small informal dinner party took place with the help of the Arbury staff, and it proved to be a very memorable occasion.

The event was repeated again the following year at the request this time of HRH Prince Phillip.

In more recent years other royals to have visited Arbury have included Princess Alice of Gloucester, sadly now deceased, and also the late Prince William of Gloucester and the present Duke of Gloucester, Prince Richard.

(B28) During this period Viscount Daventry and his two sons, the Hon. James and Hugh, would often be seen taking active part in Arbury's pheasant-shooting syndicate; all three of them were exceedingly good shots.

Soon after the autumn mists heralded the start of another season, great news was received of the birth of a son and future heir to Arbury. Humphrey John FitzRoy Newdegate was born on 23 November, first child for the Hon. James Edward and Georgia FitzRoy Newdegate, and a grandson for Viscount and Viscountess Daventry.

Church secretary of St Mary the Virgin, Harefield at this time was Mrs Jane Mennell, who spent much of her childhood at Arbury during the time of Sir Francis Alexander Newdigate-Newdegate, known as Uncle Frank.

Mrs Mennell, who is a cousin of the third Viscount Daventry, moved to Harefield in 1927 and is known locally as the last of the Newdegates.

1996

(A28) January saw the premiere of the film *Angels and Insects*, attended by Viscount Daventry, who was probably shocked at some of the sexual content. The film failed to register as more than mediocre with critics and public alike, though some of the scenes of Arbury Hall came over beautifully on the big screen.

Even though this Victorian drama left one emotionally cold, some good performances came from Mark Rylance and the very talented Kristin Scott Thomas.

Repairs and replacement stonework is an ongoing nightmare with ancient buildings and Arbury Hall is no exception.

Masons were regularly kept busy through this period with new mullions for the seventeenth-century stable block almost an annual event, and this year some of the stonework on the elaborate *Porte Cochere* was expensively replaced along the north front, with restoration work also needed on the Hall's inner courtyard chimneys.

(B40) Despite his rapidly failing health, the third Viscount Daventry somehow managed to continue his role as Lord Lieutenant of Warwickshire through to the enforced retirement age of seventy-five. This was a brave effort by the Viscount and he duly retired following seven years in office; he was succeeded by Mr Martin Dunn.

1997

Another summer quietly came and went at Arbury with the usual outdoor events, craft fairs, transport spectaculars, and corporate entertaining in the Hall. The year ended on a real high, however, with the birth of a daughter for the Hon. James Edward FitzRoy and Georgia FitzRoy Newdegate on New Year's Eve. The baby girl was named Hester Anne FitzRoy Newdegate, born on the 135th anniversary of her great-great-grandfather, Sir Francis Alexander Newdigate-Newdegate.

1998

(A37) At Harefield on 1 April, the famous hospital merged with the Royal Brompton Hospital in Chelsea to form the NHS Trust.

(B28) In July, Arbury Hall staged 'The Four Seasons' by candlelight, plus music for royal fireworks with magnificent choreographed fireworks. It proved a wonderful occasion and was attended in the park by over 5,000 spectators.

1999

Following an absence of almost seventeen years, the Newdegate family actually returned to living in Arbury Hall. During late summer the heir to the Arbury Estates, the Hon. James Edward, and Georgia FitzRoy Newdegate, along with their two children Humphrey John and Hester Anne moved to Arbury. It was the first time since the death of the Hon. Mrs L C S FitzRoy Newdegate in September 1982 that a member of the family had lived in the Hall on a permanent basis.

A tremendous amount of work was needed on the historic building to make this a reality; this work was overseen by architect Peregrine Bryant.

Mrs Sheila Stainthorpe with the Dowager Rose Lady Newdegate and the The Fourth Viscountess Daventry

During this project human remains were discovered by the Hall. Could this have been a burial ground of the Augustinian Canons of Erdbury Priory? However, this appears to have been properly dealt with by Viscount Daventry.

In his new book Simon Jenkins lists Astley Church among the top 1,000 churches in England.

2000

(A28) The year began on a very sad note with two family deaths in quick succession. At around 11 a.m. on 15 February, the third Viscount Daventry, Francis Humphrey Maurice FitzRoy Newdegate, passed away following a long illness. The Viscount's funeral at St Mary's Church, Astley on 24 February was attended by hundreds of people from all walks of life. He was succeeded by his eldest son the Hon. James Edward, who became the fourth Viscount Daventry. This very sad event was followed just a few days later by the tragic death of the Viscount's younger brother Hugh Francis, who died from a tragic accident while on a business trip to Rangoon in Burma.

Both the third Viscount and his younger son, the Hon. Hugh Francis, were buried at Arbury.

(B40) Following the death of the late Lord Daventry and the present Lord Daventry's brother Hugh Francis FitzRoy Newdegate, the family decided to create a family burial ground within the park at Arbury. The site itself was chosen near to Swanlands in a leafy paddock and the necessary planning permission was obtained.

The ground was consecrated by the Rev. John Philpott, who was vicar of Chilvers Coton and St Mary's, Astley. Soon afterwards the vicar left the parish to take up a new post as vicar of the English-speaking church in Prague.

The present Viscount Daventry took it upon himself to create a millennium project during the year, which incorporated building a swimming pool, a pool house, and landscaping the gardens within the existing kitchen walled garden. This was a major project, which took almost a year to complete, and the architect who designed the pool house was again Peregrine Bryant.

2001

A return to happier times at Arbury with the news on 8 March of the birth of a second daughter and third child to Lord and Lady Daventry, the Hon. Sophia Hebe FitzRoy Newdegate.

Towards the end of the year Lord and Lady Daventry announced their intention of making changes to some of the public rooms at Arbury – not only making it more practical for their use, but also to revitalise some parts of the hall that had remained unchanged in almost fifty years.

2002

During the closed winter season the changes took place, supervised by Mr Stuart Meese, who has looked after the Arbury painting collection for the last twenty years.

The saloon was the room that received the most attention. It was painted Sandstone, which highlighted Sir Roger's wonderful ceiling beautifully. Paintings were expertly cleaned and re-hung, some in different positions, while furniture and porcelain was re-positioned around the Hall to transform and revitalise its appearance.

The main entrance hall on the north front also received a nice new airy look and was lifted with two new portraits – one of the present owner, the fourth Viscount Daventry, and the other an impressive formal version of his late father, the third Viscount. Both portraits were executed by Marcus May.

Overall, the effect was very pleasing and Lord and Lady Daventry felt that the whole exercise had been an exciting privilege. All the work was coincidentally completed on Sophia's first birthday, in time for the new season. Since the Newdegates took up residence, the extent to which the Hall had been open to the public had also been somewhat scaled down to afford Lord and Lady Daventry more privacy to bring up their young family at Arbury.

Lord and Lady Daventry threw a party at Arbury on Tuesday, 4 June to celebrate the occasion of Queen Elizabeth's Golden Jubilee. The lovely event on a beautiful sunny afternoon was a colourful party attended by well over a hundred people, mostly dressed in patriotic colours of red, white, and blue.

Owen Stainthorpe's last big shoot, 18 January 2003

The autumn mists of November heralded the start of another pheasant-shooting season, the last before retirement for gamekeeper Owen Stainthorpe. And what a fine climax it turned out to be.

The head keeper, Owen, with Lord Daventry.
Picture courtesy of Tony Deeming.

2003

(A28) 18 January was the last big Saturday shoot for the gamekeeper, and he and assistant David Culton produced enough quality pheasants for The Guns to record the highest ever one-day bag at Arbury.

In fact it was also a record season when shooting ended on 1 February, and the keeper was honoured by a surprise party generously provided by Viscount and Viscountess Daventry.

The occasion was enjoyed by the whole of the shooting fraternity in the stable tea-rooms on the evening of the final day of the season.

When Arbury Hall opened its doors to the public on Easter Sunday it was the fiftieth anniversary of opening the Hall to visitors. So it was rather appropriate that Harefield's last known surviving Newdegate, Mrs Jane Mennell, should make a nostalgic return trip to Arbury along with the Harefield History Society on 10 June.

Now even today Arbury has very knowledgeable team of guides, but the loyal service shown by one lady in particular is quite remarkable. Mrs Kay Collier has been a guide at Arbury for the whole of that fifty-year period, a quite astonishing record – well done Kay!

Restoration seems ongoing at Arbury and this particular year proved no exception, with extensive and expensive repairs in the gardens.

(B32) During the summer the present Lord Daventry decided that there needed to be major repairs to the eighteenth-century stone pillars which run along the bee garden, as well as complete restoration of the Elizabethan red-brick wall and pillars at the northern end of the rose garden. This was a major project and took four months to complete, and was again overseen by architect Peregrine Bryant.

(C38) As the year 2003 drew to a close the fight went on to save the world-famous Harefield Hospital from the threat of closure. A fine record of more than 2,000 heart transplants, plus thousands of heart-bypass operations made one mystified at the government's intention to replace it. A protest march to Downing Street to deliver the 160,000-signature petition was led by Sophie Parks, a ten-year-old double heart transplant patient.

2004

During September, Arbury was again centre stage for a BBC episode of the detective series *Dalziel and Pascoe*. Around sixty per cent of the two-part programme was filmed at Arbury and it was shown in early February 2005.

At Astley, extensions to the reading rooms were completed making the facilities much improved with a brand new kitchen.

Harefield United reserves playing Waltham Forest at the Neudegate-owned Preston Park

Mrs Jane Mennell, the last of the Harefield Newdegates, 2005

Harefield Today

A solution to the hospital problems appears to have been resolved with the announcement that plans are being drawn up to provide the Royal Brompton and Harefield Hospitals with complete new facilities as part of the huge Paddington Basin project, which will include a brand new facility with an advanced heart and lung centre, benefiting future generations of NHS patients.

If the hospital on Harefield Park arguably remains the most important building today, the church remains the hub of the old village with its many memorials to past lords of the manor.

Close by are the Alms Houses, a memorial to the charitable one-time resident of Harefield Manor, Alice, Countess of Derby, whose will in 1637 provided for them. By the village green stands the fifteenth-century King's Arms, while on the green is Harefield's memorial to eighty of its men who fell in the first world war and thirty-one killed or missing in the second. A new organ in St Mary's in 1952 was also dedicated as a memorial to men killed in the second world war.

A special service is held on Anzac Day every year (25 April) usually attended by the Australian High Commissioner and local schoolchildren. The memorial is held at the Australian Cemetery by the church, on land originally given by Sir Francis Alexander Newdigate-Newdegate, under the shadows of an ancient yew tree. The only land in the village today still owned by the Newdegate family is the home of Harefield United Football Club, Preston Park, Breakspeare Road.

United, one of the oldest teams in England, founded back in 1868, currently perform in the Minerva Spartan South Midlands League, Premier Division.

So here in the new millennium, are there any more links with Harefield's rich history and the present FitzRoy Newdegate family? The answer is yes: the fourth Viscount Daventry, James Edward FitzRoy Newdegate is still Lord of the Manor of Harefield (Patron of the Living); long may it continue.

The ruins of Astley Castle

Astley Today

For at least a thousand years, Astley has been a very special place, though it's probably quieter now than at any time during that period, even though its roads and modern transport make it more accessible.

A casual visitor could be excused for thinking that the place is dead and derelict, with abandoned farm buildings, empty paddocks and a sadly ruined castle standing as a monument to grander times. Even the Church of St Mary the Virgin is only a shadow of its former glory. Yet it still provides the pulse of Astley village life to this day, a village community that is as special as the place itself. This has recently been reflected by the production of *The Astley Millennium Scrapbooks*, a wonderful endeavour by past and present villagers to not only raise revenue for the church, but preserve some of its golden memories for ever. The scrapbooks were lovingly collated by Jean Lapworth, Cynthia Boff, Peggy Daulman, David and Len Brandreth, Gwen Moreton, Mary Davis and many others too numerous to mention.

At services normally conducted by the Rev. Peter Brown, vicar of Chilvers Coton and Astley congregations, they tend to struggle for numbers – as do many churches, particularly in rural areas. However, two exceptions in the year at St Mary's are the harvest festival service at the end of summer and the candlelit carol service prior to Christmas. On these occasions all the hard work is often rewarded, with the church packed to the rafters.

On the strength of this closely knit community, the village fights back against the pressures of modern society. A solution still awaits the castle, but one thing is certain: Astley still retains its rare beauty and unique atmosphere as one of the most important historical sites in Warwickshire.

Long may it remain.

The Rt Hon. The Fourth Viscount Daventry attending a fund-raising event at the George Eliot Hospice, with his family and fund-raising managers, Jaqueline Biggs and Janet Griffin, November 2005. Picture by kind permission of the Heartland Evening News.

Arbury Today

Arbury in the year 2005, virtually on the 200th anniversary of the completion of Sir Roger Newdigate's Gothic Revival dream, is most definitely not without its problems.

The present owner, Lord Daventry, has had a full quinquennial report carried out and from this report it has become apparent that there need to be major repairs to the external stonework and to much of the roof of the main house. These works represent a colossal undertaking and will be carried out over the next four years.

Skilled craftsmen and materials are more costly than ever before, but it's wonderful to see Arbury with its early Gothic Revival Hall, arguably the best in England, surviving, and still the ancestral home of the Newdegates after 420 years.

Today the public still come to Arbury to enjoy its unique heritage with many private parties and corporate entertaining arriving weekly during the summer season. So, despite all of its setbacks, the show goes on, as the late third Viscount Daventry was quoted as saying at a press interview. The role of the aristocracy has changed very little; neither has the tranquil beauty of Arbury Hall.

David McGrory tells an Arbury Ghost Story

Arbury at Christmas has always been associated with ghost stories, possibly because it is the time when one year ends and another begins.

These times of endings and beginnings were always thought in the past to be a period when the borders between the natural and supernatural rubbed, allowing things to happen. This is an Arbury ghost story based on a real event.

Up until the 1860s the shattered splinter of an ancient wind-torn oak tree stood in Arbury Park, north of Coventry. The locals shunned the splinter, which consisted mainly of bark and a little wood.

Why? Well one winter's night many years earlier, when the tree was still intact, Warwickshire was battered by a terrific storm, which tore the tree from its roots.

The following morning, as a farm labourer passed by he noticed something unusual. After pulling the broken branches aside, he was shocked to uncover a disarticulated but complete skeleton.

The estate steward was informed and he in turn notified the police and the coroner.

An inquest was held but, although it was remembered that a gamekeeper had disappeared many years previously, no one could connect this with the bones, so an open verdict was recorded.

Many years passed and the incident of the bones in the tree was forgotten. That is, until an old man, an ex-ribbon weaver called Ephraim Tedds, made a deathbed confession.

He said that when he was a young man and his trade was in decline, he had resorted to a life of poaching, single-handedly decimating the game on the Newdegate estate of Arbury Hall.

He and the Arbury keepers were sworn enemies, including a young keeper called Samuel Jenkins. Samuel had been an orphan, born in Chilvers Coton College for the Poor. His mother was unmarried and had held a post at Arbury Hall.

She became pregnant and tried to drown herself in one of the ponds on the estate, but was rescued by a stable hand and placed in the college, where Samuel was born. Unfortunately, his mother died within days of his birth.

The Newdegate family placed the baby in the care of a family who farmed on the estate at Astley and, when he reached the age of eighteen years, the now strong and handsome youth was taken to Arbury Hall to learn the skills of a gamekeeper.

It is said that by the age of twenty-two Sam had become the terror of the local poachers.

Not surprisingly, he and Tedds had a great dislike for one another and one day their hatred became a public spectacle, when for a cash sum they fought bare-fisted in the Bull Ring at Chilvers Coton Wake.

Sam gave Tedds a severe beating and took the purse. As Tedds left he turned round to Sam and told him that if it were the last thing he did he would do for him. The few who heard this knew it was no idle threat, knowing Tedds' character.

On Christmas Eve, as the snow lay thick upon the ground, Sam trudged out with his dog on his evening round of the estate.

That was the last time he was ever seen alive.

A search party set out to look for him but the continuing snowfall had covered his footprints, leaving no clue.

Mr Newdegate called for a police search party and with the help of locals another search was made but again nothing was found; Sam Jenkins and his dog had disappeared.

It is said that twenty years passed and the event was forgotten, when on Christmas Eve, the anniversary of his disappearance, the bell ringers and clerk of Astley Church were returning home from carol singing and passed by the old oak.

They stopped in their tracks, for before them stood an apparition of a man blocking their path. In their panic they ran in different directions.

Few thought much of the apparition, except the landlord of Boot Inn at Chilvers Coton, who had heard the threat made by Tedds many years before.

When the tree blew down many years later, exposing the remains, it was he who pointed the finger at Tedds, although Tedds somehow managed to produce an alibi, claiming that on the night of the disappearance he was at home in bed at Heath End.

It wasn't until Christmas Eve thirty-five years later that Tedds finally confessed to the murder of Sam Jenkins.

He and Sam Jenkins had come face to face in a blizzard near the old oak. A fight ensued and Sam was beaten down, dead or unconscious.

Tedds took Jenkins' body to the oak. He knew it had a hollow in the crown, which he sometimes used to hide game.

He heaved the body into it and packed it with snow, planning that when it melted he would conceal it better. Sam's faithful dog wouldn't leave the spot, so Tedds killed it. The dog was then thrown down a nearby coal pit shaft.

It was said afterwards that, on several Christmas Eves, a cottager who lived nearby heard the howls of a dog in distress by the wind-torn oak, but on checking never found anything...

Arbury Hall across the garden pool

Custodians of Arbury

	Life span	Ownership
Sir Edmund Anderson	1530–1605	1567–1586
John Newdegate	1541–1592	1586–1587
Sir John Newdegate	1571–1610	1587–1610
John Newdegate	1600–1642	1610–1642
Sir Richard Newdigate, first Bart	1602–1678	1642–1665
Sir Richard Newdigate, second Bart	1644–1710	1665–1710
Sir Richard Newdigate, third Bart	1668–1727	1710–1727
Sir Edward Newdigate, fourth Bart	1715–1734	1727–1734
Sir Roger Newdigate, fifth Bart	1719–1806	1734–1806
Francis Parker Newdigate	1765–1835	1806–1835
The Rt Hon. Charles Newdigate-Newdegate	1816–1887	1835–1887
Lt Gen. Sir Edward Newdigate-Newdegate	1825–1902	1887–1902
Sir Francis Alexander Newdigate-Newdegate	1862–1936	1902–1936
The Hon. Mrs Lucia FitzRoy-Newdegate	1896–1982	1936–1950
Third Viscount Daventry F H M FitzRoy Newdegate	1921–2000	1950–2000
Fourth Viscount Daventry James Edward FitzRoy-Newdegate	1960–	2000–

Notes on Sources and Inspiration

The inspiration for completing these chronicles came from wanting to put to good use all the accumulating personal knowledge gained over many years of studying local history.

This includes the wealth of previously published in-depth accounts on various issues and the lifetimes of very important and interesting people.

Many of the public figures written about in these chronicles are the subjects of in-depth studies so wonderfully researched and portrayed by such authors as V M Larminie with *The Godly Magistrate*, and Eileen Gooder with her marvellous production of *The Squire of Arbury*.

Another source of stimulation came from the wonderful production of *The Correspondence of Sir Roger Newdigate of Arbury*, under the general editorship of Joan Lane MA, PLD, FSA. Both of these are Dugdale Society productions.

The Cheverals of Cheveral Manor by Lady Newdigate-Newdegate, published in 1898, is another brilliant inside account of the life and times of Sir Christopher Cheveral (George Eliot's pseudonym for Sir Roger Newdigate).

Both *The Princes in the Tower* and *Elizabeth* by Allison Weir and David Starkey respectively are stimulating and stirring accounts of the fifteenth and sixteenth centuries. Some of David's powerfully brilliant words are quoted in the section on 1553.

With local knowledge, both published and unpublished, spread over such a wide playing field, the temptation to produce an attractive reference book became apparent. *The Chronicles of the Newdegates and the Three Manors* describes much of our wonderful and bloody past, revealing what really happened and when, but largely in a brief text.

Most quotes are covered in the text itself, while personal memories and knowledge are passed on with loving enthusiasm.

The skirmish at Astley Castle during the Civil War, referred to in the entry for 1646, may have been the result of the ongoing feud between two of Leicestershire's most powerful families, the Greys and Hastings.

These families were very often on opposing sides in major and minor conflicts over the centuries, while Astley had once belonged to the Greys.

Sir Richard Newdigate, the first Baronet, is often referred to as the Sergeant, which not only maintains the wonderful idea by Eileen Gooder, but gives clear reference to father Richard who shares the same name as his son the second Baronet.

Bibliography and Key for References and Inspiration

How the Bibliography works

Where the year is divided into more than one reference source, the numbers equate to the key below, p. 161–163. If there is only one source of reference for a particular year, then that is the source shown in the Source Index (p.163).

1. *Domesday Book*
2. Branston, W K, *The Story of the Parish Church of St Mary the Virgin*, Astley, Atherstone, Baxters, 1963
3. Goatman, Wilfred, *Harefield and her Church*, Twickenham, Riverside Press, 1947, revised 1972
4. Moorman, John, MADD, *Lanercoste Priory* (Guidebook), Gilsland, Cumbria & Kingsley, Hants., Pacific Press
5. Veasey, E A, *Nuneaton: A History*, Chichester, Phillimore & Co Ltd
6. Weir, Allison, *The Princes in the Tower*, London, Bodley Head, 1992
7. Larminie, V M, *The Godly Magistrate*, Oxford, The Dugdale Society, 1982
8. Carr-Gregg Mafras, Rev. Ivo, Vicar of Astley, *History of Astley*, Herald Press, 1930
9. *Pears Cyclopaedia*, ninetieth edition, Pelham Books, 1981
10. Starkey, David, *Elizabeth*, London, Vintage, 2001
11. Rowse, A L, *The England of Elizabeth*, London, Macmillan, 1950, 1953
12. Gooder, Eileen, *The Squire of Arbury*, Coventry, The Historical Society

13. Smith, Christopher, 'Sir Walter Raleigh', at http://www.britannia.com/bios/raleigh/out.html

14. Church History, Kelly's Directory, Bedfordshire, 1898. http://www.genuki.org.uk/big/eng/bdf/eyeworth

15. Guide's Information, Arbury Hall, by kind permission of the fourth Viscount Daventry

16. Dugdale, Sir William, *Antiquaries of Warwick*, vol. II, Manchester, E J Morten Ltd

17. Lane, Joan, MA, PhD, FSA, editor, *The Correspondence of Sir Roger Newdigate of Arbury*, Warwickshire, Hertfordshire, The Dugdale Society, 1995

18. Fordham, D N, *Industrial History of Arbury*, unpublished thesis

19. Adams, Kathleen, *George Eliot County*, fifth edition, Nuneaton, Albion Press, 1988

20. Stevenson, Joan, *The Greys of Bradgate*, Leicester, Bradgate Books, 1974

21. Newdigate-Newdegate, Lady, *The Cheverals of Cheveral Manor*, London, Longmans Green & Co., 1898

22. References supplied by the fourth Viscount Daventry

23. http://www.genuki.org.uk/big/eng/bdf/Eyeworth/

24. Sassoon, Seigfreid, *Memoirs of a Fox Hunting Man*, London, Faber & Faber, 1928

25. *The Field* magazine, London, Burlington Publishing Co. Ltd

26. *Girls Own* magazine/newspaper, vol. XIII, No. 639, March 26 1892

27. http://www.allsydney.com/west/newdegat.htm

28. Personal knowledge and local information acquired during the author's lifetime

29. *Astley Millennium Scrapbook*, unpublished

30. 'Oxford Poetry, appendix two: the Newdigate Prize', http://www.gnelson.demon.uk/oxpoetry/index/1newo.htlm.

31. Coton Church, commemorative pamphlet (pew leaflet) issued for the Coton Festival, 1941/1991

32. *BBC History* magazine, vol. 4, No. 2, BBC Worldwide Ltd, February 2003

33. http://www.Westminster-abbey.org/stmargarets/guide/south-aisle.htm

35. Tyack, Geoffrey, *Warwickshire Country Houses in the Age of Classicism, 1650–1680*, Warwickshire Local History Society, occasional papers No. 3, 1980

36. Beckles, Gordon, *Coronation Souvenir Book 1937*, London, a Daily Express publication, 1937

37. Royal Brompton & Harefield NHS Trust, http://www.rbh. Nthames.nhs.uk/internetsection/about/about.asp

38. *Heartland Evening News*, 25 July 2003

39. McGrory, David, historian to the Coventry Evening Telegraph, 'Ghost Story'

40. Fourth Viscount Daventry

41. http://www.rbh.nth.nhs.uk/internetsection/about/PaddingtonOverview

Source Index

1492	(6)	1607	(8)
1535	(3)	1608	(3)
1536	(5)	1610	(3)
1538	(15)	1617	(3)
1539	(15)	1618	(15)
1541	(15)	1620	(12)
1545	(2)	1628	(15)
1551	(8)	1632	(12)
1553	(10)	1637	(3)
1554	(10)A&B(15)C(8)	1642	(15)
1555	(2)	1642–1643	(12)
1559	(3)	1644	(12)
1567	(15)	1646	(16)
1571	(15)	1648	(12)
1575	(15)	1649	(12A(3)B
1577	(15)	1654	(12)A(8)B
1581	(23)	1655	(3)A(12)B
1582	(15)	1657	(12)
1584	(15)	1658	(15)
1585	(15)	1660	(15)A(3)B
1586	(15)	1661	(12)
1587	(12)(7)A B	1665	(12)A(15)B
1588	(23)	1666	(12)
1592	(7)	1668	(12)A(15)B
1594	(23)	1674	(3)A (15)B
1595	(11)	1675	(12)
1599	(11)	1676	(8)
1600	A(7) B (8) (3)C	1677	(15)
1601	(3)A(7)B	1678	(15)
1602	(3)A(12)B	1680	(12)
1603	(7)A(14)B(3)C	1681	(15)
1605	(14) A (23)B	1683	(12)
1606	(7)	1684	(12)

1685	(15)	1760	(3)A(17)B
1689	(15)	1761	(18)
1691	12)	1762	(15)
1692	(15)	1764	(15)
1694	(12)	1765	(15)A(18)B
1695	(12)	1766	(17)
1699	(12)	1768	(3)
1703	(12)	1769	(17)
1704	(12)	1770	(17)A (18)B
1703	(12)	1771	(18)
1710	(15)	1772	(18)
1711	(15)	1773	(17)
1712	(12)	1774	(15)A(17)B
1715	(12)	1776	(17)
1719	(15)	1778	(15)
1727	(3)	1779	(18)
1730	(12)	1780	(17)A(3)B
1732	(15)	1781	(15)
1734	(15)	1782	(18)
1736	(17)	1783	(18)A(15)B
1738	(17)	1784	(18)
1739	(17)	1785	(18)
1740	(17)	1786	(18)A&C(15)B
1742	(15)	1787	(15)A(8)B(3)C
1743	(15)	1790	(15)
1745	(15)	1791	(15)
1747	(17)	1792–1793	(18)
1749	(3)	1795	(17)A(15)B
1750	(15)	1797	(17)
1751	(17)	1800	(15)
1752	(3)A(17)B	1803	(15
1756	(15)	1805	(17)
1758	(17)	1806	(15)

1809	(8)	1891	(15)
1813	(19)A(3)B	1892	(15)
1816	(15)	1893	(15)
1819	(19)	1896	(15)
1820	(8)	1897	(15)
1825	(15)	1898	(3)A(22)B
1832	(19)A(3)B(15)C	1899	(20)
1835	(15)	1901	(15)A(9)B
1837	(15)	1902	(15)
1841	(3)	1903	(8)
1843	(15)	1905	(8)A(15)B
1845	(8)	1906	(22)
1848	(27)	1909	(15)
1850	(5)	1910	(8)
1851	(20)	1914	(3)
1854	(9)A(15)B–D(8)C(15)D	1915	(3)
		1917	(15)A(3)B(15)C
1855	(8)	1918	(3)
1857	(19)	1919	(3)A(15)B
1862	(15)	1920	(15)A(3)B
1866	(15)	1921	(15)A(3)B
1870	(20)	1924	(15)
1872	(15)	1925	(15)
1874	(8)	1926	(3)A(27)B(15)C
1875	(8)	1927	((8)A(15)B
1878	(8)A(30)B	1928	(24)
1879	(15)	1929	(15)
1880	(3)A(19)B(22)C	1930	(15)
1882	(15)	1934	(22)
1885	(15)	1935	(15)
1886	(22)	1936	(15)A(36)B
1887	(15)	1939	(15)
1888	(15)	1940	(15)

1941	(22)	1973	(29)A(30)B
1942	(22)	1972–1978	(30)
1943	(34)A(28)B	1975/1976	(28)
1945	(28)	1978	(28)
1946	(28)A(31)B	1981	(28)
1947	(31)A(28)B	1982	(15)A(28)B(30)C
1950	(28)	1984	(15)
1951	(3)A(29)B	1986	(28)
1952	(2)A(9)B	1987	(28)
1953	(15)A(28)B	1990	(28)A(30)B
1955	(22)	1992–1995	(30)
1956	(29)	1994	(28)
1958	(29)	1995	(40)A(28)B
1959	(28)	1996	(28)A(40)B
1960	(2)A(28)B	1997	(28)
	(30)C(3)D(28)E	1998	((37)A (28)B
1961–1962	(2)A(28)B	1999	(28)
1962	(28)	2000	(28)A(40)B
1964	(28)	2001	(28)
1965	(28)A(30)B	2002	(28)
1968	(30)	2003	(28A(32)B(38)C
1969	(29)	2004	(28)
1970	(28)		
1971	(28)		

Photographic Credits

Photographs on p.2, 5, 32, 40, 41, 50, 61, 66, 67, 70, 71, 76, 77, 88, 89, 99, 103, 106, 116, 117, 157 by kind permission of the Rt Hon. The Fourth Viscount Daventry.

Photograph on p.8 by kind permission of Mrs Sylvia Wilkinson.

Photograph on p.152 by kind permission of the *Heartland Evening News*.

Pictures on p. 108 and 109 by kind permission of Miss Jean Lapworth.

Photograph on p.145 by kind permission of Mr Tony Deeming.

Photograph on p.7 by kind permission of Mr Hugo Burnand.

Photographs on p.17, 22, 27, 28, 35, 42, 43, 46, 47, 55, 56, 80, 81, 82, 84, 85, 94, 96, 102, 123, 126, 131, 141, 144, 147, 148, 150 by Roy Wilkinson.

Printed in the United Kingdom
by Lightning Source UK Ltd.
116414UKS00001B/133-201